THE KEY
STUDENT STUDY GU

Canadian History 10 Applied (CHC2P)

THE KEY student study guide is designed to help students achieve success in school. The content in each study guide is 100% curriculum aligned and serves as an excellent source of material for review and practice. To create this book, teachers, curriculum specialists, and assessment experts have worked closely to develop the instructional pieces that explain each of the key concepts for the course. The practice questions and sample tests have detailed solutions that show problem-solving methods, highlight concepts that are likely to be tested, and point out potential sources of errors. **THE KEY** is a complete guide to be used by students throughout the school year for reviewing and understanding course content, and to prepare for assessments.

Published 2008
Copyright © 2008 by Castle Rock Research Corp.

Rao, Gautam, 1961 –
THE KEY –Canadian History 10 Applied (2009 Edition) Ontario

1. Canadian History – Juvenile Literature. I. Title

Published by
Castle Rock Research Corp.
2340 Manulife Place
10180 – 101 Street
Edmonton, AB T5J 3S4

1 2 3 FP 10 09 08

Printed in Canada

Publisher
Gautam Rao

Contributors
Brigitta Braden
Kelly Drury-Laffin

Dedicated to the memory of Dr. V. S. Rao

THE KEY—Canadian History Applied Grade 10

THE KEY consists of the following sections:

KEY Tips for Being Successful at School gives examples of study and review strategies. It includes information about learning styles, study schedules, and note taking for test preparation.

Class Focus includes a unit on each area of the curriculum. Units are divided into sections, each focusing on one of the specific expectations, or main ideas, that students must learn about in that unit. Examples, definitions, and visuals help to explain each main idea. Practice questions on the main ideas are also included. At the end of each unit is a test on the important ideas covered. The practice questions and unit tests help students identify areas they know and those they need to study more. They can also be used as preparation for tests and quizzes. Most questions are of average difficulty, though some are easy and some are hard—the harder questions are called *Challenger Questions*. Each unit is prefaced by a *Table of Correlations,* which correlates questions in the unit (and in the practice tests at the end of the book) to the specific curriculum expectations. Answers and solutions are found at the end of each unit.

KEY Strategies for Success on Tests helps students get ready for tests. It shows students different types of questions they might see, word clues to look for when reading them, and hints for answering them.

Practice Tests includes one to three tests based on the entire course. They are very similar to the format and level of difficulty that students may encounter on final tests. In some regions, these tests may be reprinted versions of official tests, or reflect the same difficulty levels and formats as official versions. This gives students the chance to practice using real-world examples. Answers and complete solutions are provided at the end of the section.

For the complete curriculum document (including specific expectations along with examples and sample problems), visit www.edu.gov.on.ca/eng/curriculum/secondary.

THE KEY Study Guides are available for many courses. Check www.castlerockresearch.com for a complete listing of books available for your area.

For information about any of our resources or services, please call Castle Rock Research at 905.625.3332 or visit our website at http://www.castlerockresearch.com.

At Castle Rock Research, we strive to produce an error-free resource. If you should find an error, please contact us so that future editions can be corrected.

TABLE OF CONTENTS

NOTES

KEY Tips for Being Successful at School

KEY FACTORS CONTRIBUTING TO SCHOOL SUCCESS

In addition to learning the content of your courses, there are some other things that you can do to help you do your best at school. Some of these strategies are listed below.

- **KEEP A POSITIVE ATTITUDE.** Always reflect on what you can already do and what you already know.

- **BE PREPARED TO LEARN.** Have ready the necessary pencils, pens, notebooks, and other required materials for participating in class.

- **COMPLETE ALL OF YOUR ASSIGNMENTS.** Do your best to finish all of your assignments. Even if you know the material well, practice will reinforce your knowledge. If an assignment or question is difficult for you, work through it as far as you can so that your teacher can see exactly where you are having difficulty.

- **SET SMALL GOALS** for yourself when you are learning new material. For example, when learning the parts of speech, do not try to learn everything in one night. Work on only one part or section each study session. When you have memorized one particular part of speech and understand it, then move on to another one, continue this process until you have memorized and learned all the parts of speech.

- **REVIEW YOUR CLASSROOM WORK** regularly at home to be sure that you understand the material that you learned in class.

- **ASK YOUR TEACHER FOR HELP** when you do not understand something or when you are having a difficult time completing your assignments.

- **GET PLENTY OF REST AND EXERCISE.** Concentrating in class is hard work. It is important to be well-rested and have time to relax and socialize with your friends. This helps you to keep a positive attitude about your school work.

- **EAT HEALTHY MEALS** A balanced diet keeps you healthy and gives you the energy that you need for studying at school and at home.

HOW TO FIND YOUR LEARNING STYLE

Every student has a certain manner in which it seems easier for him or her to learn. The manner in which you learn best is called your learning style. By knowing your learning style, you can increase your success at school. Most students use a combination of learning styles. Do you know what type of learner you are? Read the following descriptions. Which of these common learning styles do you use most often?

Linguistic Learner: You may learn best by saying, hearing, and seeing words. You are probably really good at memorizing things such as dates, places, names, and facts. You may need **to write and then say out loud** the steps in a process, a formula, or the actions that lead up to a significant event.

Spatial Learner: You may learn best by looking at and working with pictures. You are probably really good at puzzles, imagining things, and reading maps and charts. You may need to use strategies like **mind mapping and webbing** to organize your information and study notes.

Kinaesthetic Learner: You may learn best by touching, moving, and figuring things out using manipulation. You are probably really good at physical activities and learning through movement. You may need to **draw your finger over a diagram** to remember it, **"tap out" the steps** needed to solve a problem, or **"feel" yourself writing** or typing a formula.

SCHEDULING STUDY TIME

You should review your class notes regularly to ensure that you have a clear understanding of all the new material you learned. Reviewing your lessons on a regular basis helps you to learn and remember ideas and concepts. It also reduces the quantity of material that you need to study prior to a test. Establishing a study schedule will help you to make the best use of your time.

Regardless of the type of study schedule you use, you may want to consider the following suggestions to maximize your study time and effort:

• Organize your work so that you begin with the most challenging material first.

• Divide the subject's content into small, manageable chunks.

• Alternate regularly between your different subjects and types of study activities in order to maintain your interest and motivation.

• Make a daily list with headings like "Must Do," "Should Do," and "Could Do."

• Begin each study session by quickly reviewing what you studied the day before.

• Maintain a routine of eating, sleeping, and exercising to help you concentrate better for extended periods of time.

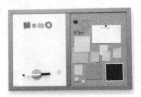

CREATING STUDY NOTES

MIND-MAPPING OR WEBBING

- Use the key words, ideas, or concepts from your reading or class notes to create a *mind map* or *web* (a diagram or visual representation of the given information). A mind map or web is sometimes referred to as a *knowledge map*.

- Write the key word, concept, theory, or formula in the centre of your page.

- Write down related facts, ideas, events, and information and then link them to the central concept with lines.

- Use coloured markers, underlining, or other symbols to emphasize important information, such as relationships between ideas or specific aspects of a timeline.

The following mind map is an example of an organization tool that could help you develop an essay:

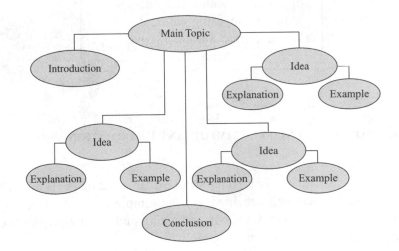

INDEX CARDS

To use index cards while studying, follow these steps:

• Write a key word or question on one side of an index card.

• On the reverse side, write the definition of the word, answer to the question, and any other important information that you want to remember.

> **What is Imperialism?**

> **What is Imperialism?**
> Imperialism is the forceful extension of a nation's authority by conquest therby imposing political and economic domination over other nations.

SYMBOLS AND STICKY NOTES—IDENTIFYING IMPORTANT INFORMATION

• Use symbols to mark your class notes. For example, an exclamation mark (!) might be used to point out something that must be learned well because it is a very important idea. A question mark(?) may highlight something that you are not certain about, and a diamond (◊) or asterisk (*) could highlight interesting information that you want to remember.

• Use sticky notes when you are not allowed to put marks in books.

• Use sticky notes to mark a page in a book that contains an important diagram, formula, explanation, etc.

• Use sticky notes to mark important facts in research books.

MEMORIZATION TECHNIQUES

- **ASSOCIATION** relates new learning to something you already know. For example, to remember the spelling difference between *dessert* and *desert*, recall that the word *sand* has only one *–s*. So, because there is sand in a desert, the word *desert* only has one *–s*.

- **MNEMONIC DEVICES** are sentences that you create to remember a list or group of items. For example, the first letter of each word in the phrase "**E**very **G**ood **B**oy **D**eserves **F**udge" helps you to remember the names of the lines on the treble clef staff (E, G, B, D, and F) in music.

- **ACRONYMS** are words that are formed from the first letters or parts of the words in a group. For example, *radar* is actually an acronym for <u>Ra</u>dio <u>De</u>tection <u>a</u>nd <u>R</u>anging, and *MASH* is an acronym for <u>M</u>obile <u>A</u>rmy <u>S</u>urgical <u>H</u>ospital. **HOMES** helps you to remember the names of the five Great Lakes (**H**uron, **O**ntario, **M**ichigan, **E**rie, and **S**uperior)

- **VISUALIZING** requires you to use your mind's eye to imagine a chart, list, map, diagram, or sentence as it is in your textbook or notes, on the chalk board or computer screen, or in a display.

- **INITIALISMS** are abbreviations that are formed from the first letters or parts of the words in a group. Unlike acronyms, initialisms cannot be pronounced as a word themselves. For example, IBM is an initialism for International Business Machines, and PRC is an initialism for the People's Republic of China.

KEY STRATEGIES FOR REVIEWING

Reviewing textbook material, class notes, and handouts should be an ongoing activity. Spending time reviewing becomes more critical when you are preparing for tests. You may find some of the following review strategies useful when studying during your scheduled study time.

- Before reading a selection, preview it by noting the headings, charts, graphs, and chapter questions.

- Read the complete introduction to identify the key information that is addressed in the selection.

- Read the first sentence of the next paragraph for the main idea.

- Skim the paragraph and make note of key words, phrases, and information.

- Read the last sentence of the paragraph.

- Repeat this process for each paragraph and section until you have skimmed the entire selection.

KEY STRATEGIES FOR SUCCESS: A CHECKLIST

Review, review, review: review is a huge part of doing well at school and preparing for tests. Here is a checklist for you to keep track of how many suggested strategies for success you are using. Read each question and then put a check mark (✓) in the correct column. Look at the questions where you have checked the "No" column. Think about how you might try using some of these strategies to help you do your best at school.

KEY Strategies for Success	Yes	No
Do you know your personal learning style—how you learn best?		
Do you spend 15 to 30 minutes a day reviewing your notes?		
Do you study in a quiet place at home?		
Do you clearly mark the most important ideas in your study notes?		
Do you use sticky notes to mark texts and research books?		
Do you practise answering multiple-choice and written-response questions?		
Do you ask your teacher for help when you need it?		
Are you maintaining a healthy diet and sleep routine?		
Are you participating in regular physical activity?		

Class Focus

Communities:

Local, National, and Global

TABLE OF CORRELATIONS				
Strand	**General Expectation**	**Specific Outcome**	**Practice Questions**	**Unit Test**
1. Communities: Local, national, and Global	1.1 describe some of the major local, national, and global forces and events that have influenced Canada's policies and Canadian identity since 1914	1.1.1 describe some of the policies championed by political leaders since 1914 that have contributed to a sense of Canadian identity	1, 5, 11, 25	1, 14
		1.1.2 identify the contributions made by selected regional, provincial, linguistic, ethnic, and/or religious communities to Canada's multicultural society	10, 22, 23, 29	
		1.1.3 describe how Canada's participation in selected world events and contributions to international organizations and agreements have contributed to an evolving sense of national identity	12, 13, 26	5, 16, 17
		1.1.4 identify some of the ways in which foreign power have influenced Canadian foreign policy	17	15
		1.1.5 describe some aspects of the impact in Canada of the experience and memory of the Holocaust		
		1.1.6 explain how American culture and lifestyles have influenced Canada and Canadians in selected periods	21	

	1.2 explain the significance of some key individuals and events in the evolution of French-English relations in Canada since 1914	1.2.1 explain why conscription was a controversial issue and how it divided English Canada and Quebec during the World War I and World War II	4,15	6
		1.2.2 identify some major events that contributed to the growth of Quebec nationalism and the separatist movement in Quebec from 1945	20, 24	8, 20
		1.2.3 describe key responses by Canadians and their political leaders to the Quebec separatist movement	19	4, 7, 9
		1.2.4 identify the major groups of French Canadians outside Quebec and describe some of their efforts to achieve recognition		
	1.3 evaluate Canada's participation in war and contributions to peacekeeping and security	1.3.1 identify the causes of World War I and World War II and explain how Canada became involved in these two wars	2, 3, 6, 16	10
		1.3.2 describe some of the contributions Canada and Canadians made to the war effort overseas during World War I and World War II	8, 18, 27	12, 13, 19
		1.3.3 describe some of the contributions Canada and Canadians made to the war effort at home during World War I and World War II, as well as some of the effects the wars had on the home from	7, 14	

Class Focus		1.3.4 describe the events leading up to the Holocaust and assess Canada's response to those events		11
		1.3.5 summarize Canada's role in some key Cold war activities from 1945 to 1989	9, 28	
		1.3.6 assess some examples of the roles and functions of the Canadian armed forces since 1945, such as peacekeeping and peace making and maintaining security	30	2, 3, 18

COMMUNITIES: LOCAL, NATIONAL, AND GLOBAL

FORCES SHAPING CANADA'S POLICIES AND CANADIAN IDENTITY

1.1.1   describe some of the policies championed by political leaders since 1914 that have contributed to a sense of Canadian identity

A COMMON CANADIAN IDENTITY

- **Policies:** High-level overall plans embracing the general goals and acceptable procedures of an organization, especially a governmental body.
- **Institutions:** Organizations dedicated to a specific purpose.

After World War I, Canada wanted to distinguish itself as a nation separate from Britain and the United States. Political leaders over the last several decades have created "made in Canada" institutions and policies to help contribute to the Canadian identity.

Legislation such as the Canadian Bill of Rights (1960), the Charter of Rights and Freedoms (1982), and the Canada Health Act (1984) are examples of laws that contribute to a sense of Canadian identity.

1.1.2   identify the contributions made by selected regional, provincial, linguistic, ethnic, and/or religious communities to Canada's multicultural society

CANADA'S MULTICULTURAL SOCIETY

- **Multicultural society:** A society containing many different cultural groups, each making up a significant percentage of the population.
- **Linguistic group:** People who share the same mother tongue (first language).
- **Ethnocultural group:** People who share similar national, tribal, or linguistic origins.
- **Religious group**: People who share the same faith.
- **Sovereign Nation:** An independent country.
- **Heterogeneous population:** A population made up of many different cultural, ethnic, and religious groups.

Many different qualities make up Canadian identity. There are numerous ethnocultural, religious, and linguistic groups that create the multicultural society of Canada. These groups have all made important contributions to the development and growth of Canada as a sovereign nation. Canada has a heterogeneous population. Other than Aboriginal peoples, all Canadians originally came from other parts of the world. The two official languages in Canada are English and French. Canadian law allows people to conduct their legal and business affairs in almost any language they choose.

There are many men and women from different cultural, racial, and ethnic backgrounds who have played major roles in shaping the Canadian identity. For example, in 1968, Ontario-born Lincoln Alexander, became the first black Canadian to sit in the House of Commons, and in 1985, he became Canada's first black lieutenant governor. Native Canadians such as artist Daphne Odjig; Elijah Harper, the first Aboriginal to be elected to a provincial (Manitoba) legislature; and Métis architect Douglas Cardinal have achieved acclaim for their contributions to Canada. Austrian-born industrialist Frank Stronach immigrated to Ontario in 1954 and became a billionaire employing well over 80 000 people.

1.1.3   describe how Canada's participation in selected world events and contributions to international organizations and agreements

CANADA'S EVOLVING IDENTITY

- **United Nations:** In 1945, representatives of 50 countries met in San Francisco at the United Nations Conference on International Organization to draw up the United Nations Charter. The Organization officially came into existence on October 24, 1945, when the Charter had been ratified by China, France, the Soviet Union, the United Kingdom, the United States, and a majority of other signatories. United Nations Day is celebrated on 24 October.

- **NATO:** An alliance of 26 countries from North America and Europe committed to fulfilling the goals of the North Atlantic Treaty signed on April 4, 1949.

- **Universal Declaration of Human Rights:** The basic international pronouncement of the inalienable and inviolable rights of all members of the human family. The Declaration was proclaimed in a resolution of the United Nations General Assembly on December 10, 1948 as the "common standard of achievement for all peoples and all nations" in respect of human rights. It lists numerous rights—civil, political, economic, social, and cultural—to which people everywhere are entitled.

Canada was one of the first nations to join the United Nations (UN) in 1945 and has played a major role in UN peacekeeping and peacemaking missions. As well, Canada participates actively in many UN agencies that focus on raising standards of living and quality of life in the developing world.

Canada also proposed an alliance of democratic nations in the North Atlantic region (NATO, 1949) in hopes of influencing American defence policy and discouraging the Soviet Union in Western Europe. Canada continues to play an active role in NATO, contributing funding, equipment and personnel, to assist with NATO's objectives.

A Canadian, John Humphrey, wrote the Universal Declaration of Human Rights, which was signed by representatives from around the world in 1948. This declaration became the basis for Canada's Charter of Rights and Freedoms, and Canada continues to be a world leader for human rights.

In the 1990s, the Canadian government agreed to the Kyoto Protocol, an international agreement designed to reduce greenhouse gas emissions.

1.1.4   identify some of the ways in which foreign powers have influenced Canadian foreign policy

CANADA'S PARTICIPATION IN WAR AND PEACEKEEPING

- **Foreign Policy:** The policy of a sovereign state in its interaction with other sovereign states.
- **Sovereignty**: In regards to countries and nations, sovereignty is the ability of a nation to have freedom from external control.

When World War I began in August 1914, Canada was still a part of the British Empire, so when Britain declared war on the Central Powers*, Canada was automatically drawn into the war as well. Canada gained complete sovereignty as a nation in 1931, so the decision to enter World War II was "made in Canada."

As a sovereign nation, Canada has become a member of the United Nations and NATO, strengthening its ties to the United States and Europe. These memberships and ties, both economic and political, greatly influence Canada's foreign policy. Canada has participated in both peacekeeping and peacemaking missions as a member of the United Nations and NATO.

1.1.5   describe some aspects of the impact in Canada of the experience and memory of the Holocaust

CANADA AND THE HOLOCAUST

- **Genocide/ethnic cleansing:** The systematic elimination, usually violently, of a national, racial, or cultural group.
- **International War Crimes Tribunals**: Courts created to try people charged with war crimes.
- **Anti-Semitism**: Hostility toward or discrimination against Jews as a religious, ethnic, or racial group

German Chancellor Adolf Hitler and his Nazi party believed that the German race was superior to Jewish people and to other groups of people, including Slavic peoples (Russians, Poles, and others). The Nazis also persecuted other groups of people based on political, behavioural, and ideological grounds, including Communists, Socialists, Jehovah's Witnesses, and homosexuals. During World War II, the Holocaust occurred in Germany with the horrific murder of 6 million Jews and 5 million other peoples that the Nazis had deemed "racially inferior."

During World War II, there were groups of Hitler supporters throughout Canada who created their own fascist organizations that supported similar ideals to those of Hitler's Nazis. Anti-Semitism and discrimination against Jews occurred across Canada. Canada's immigration policies during World War II were not friendly toward Jewish people. Following World War II, Canada became involved in the Nuremberg Trials, where Nazi war criminals were put on trial for violating the rules of war.

Canada has tried to prevent incidents of genocide/ethnic cleansing in the African country of Rwanda and the former Yugoslavia in the 1990s by sending in peacekeepers. Also in the 1990s, Canadian Louise Arbour served as the United Nations chief prosecutor at the International War Crimes Tribunals. These courts were created to try people charged with war crimes against humanity in both Rwanda and the former Yugoslavia.

Two examples of laws created to protect the human rights of Canadians are the Canadian Bill of Rights (1960) and the Charter of Rights and Freedoms (1982).

1.1.6 explain how American culture and lifestyles have influenced Canada and Canadians in selected periods

AMERICAN INFLUENCE

- **Culture**: The behaviour and beliefs of a group of people.
- **Lifestyles:** The typical way of life of an individual, group, or culture.

Canada is heavily influenced by the United States, which has 10 times the population of Canada. Many of the movies, television programs, and magazines that Canadians are exposed to come from the U.S. The Canadian government has created and funded institutions to protect and promote Canadian culture. The federal government has created several national institutions such as the Canadian Broadcasting Corporation (CBC), the National Film Board (NFB), and the Canadian Radio–Television and Telecommunications Commission (CRTC).

These groups try to protect and promote Canadian culture. CBC Radio, created in 1936, focuses on giving Canadians mostly Canadian news and entertainment. Established in 1968, the CRTC ensures that at least 50 percent of prime time programming on radio or television has Canadian content.

FRENCH-ENGLISH RELATIONS

1.2.1   explain why conscription was a controversial issue and how it divided English Canada and Quebec during World War I and World War II

CONSCRIPTION CAUSING TENSIONS

• **Conscription:** Forced military service.

Tensions between English and French Canada increased during World Wars I and II because of the conflict in beliefs regarding Canada's participation in these wars. Canada was a nation divided by World War I. At the beginning in 1914, there was a flood of volunteers to serve in the war, but these were mostly English Canadians eager to support Britain. By 1916, the number of volunteers began to decrease, yet Canada's prime minister, Robert Borden, vowed to send even more troops. To fulfill his promise, he needed to enact a policy of conscription. This policy was not supported by French Canadians, and some others, who were reluctant to participate. Conscription became the main issue in the 1917 election. Borden's Union government won the election; however, 62 of 65 Quebec seats went to Wilfrid Laurier and the Liberals who opposed conscription. The Military Service Act of 1917 introduced conscription and further increased tensions between Quebec and the rest of Canada.

At the start of World War II, Canada was still dealing with the tensions created by the World War I conscription crisis, so Prime Minister Mackenzie King vowed that no Canadians would be conscripted to fight in this war. Near the end of the war, King did conscript several thousand Canadians to serve overseas, but because Quebec cabinet minister Louis St. Laurent supported Prime Minister King's conscription policies, the tension levels in Quebec did not reach those of World War I.

1.2.2   identify some major events that contributed to the growth of Quebec nationalism and the separatist movement in Quebec from 1945

1.2.3   describe key responses by Canadians and their political leaders to the Quebec separatist movement

QUEBEC NATIONALISM

• **Nationalism:** A set of principles or a political movement that promotes a nation's political autonomy and national identity based on a shared history or culture, often identified on the grounds of race or ethnicity.

• **Quiet Revolution:** A time in the 1960s when Quebecers were promoting pride in French-Canadian language and culture.

• **Nationalize:** To put a private industry or assets under government ownership.

• **Separatists:** People who want an independent Quebec.

• **Referendum**: A direct vote by citizens on an issue.

• **Sovereignty association:** The concept that Quebec could be an independent country with strong economic ties to the rest of Canada.

• **Federalism**: The concept of Quebec remaining part of Canada.

Maurice Duplessis was Quebec's premier for most of the years between the mid-1930s until 1959. He wanted to preserve the French language, religion, and way of life in Quebec, and to do so, he believed that he needed to avoid the English influence of the federal government.

By the 1960s, Quebecers had become less rural and more urban; they were also becoming more secular (non-religious). As Quebec society changed, the political landscape began to change as well. Liberal premier Jean Lesage made sweeping changes to give his provincial government more control than the federal government, beginning the Quiet Revolution. Using the slogan "*maître chez nous*," or masters in our own home, the Lesage régime began to modernize the economy and nationalize (for Quebec) industries formerly owned by English Canadians and Americans.

While Lesage and others wanted to remain a part of Canada, with "special status," there were other groups who wanted more independence; these groups became known as separatists. In the 1960s, the *Front de Libération du Québec* (FLQ) and the Parti Québécois (PQ) emerged with the goal of separating Quebec from Canada. The FLQ used violence, most notably in what is now called the October Crisis (1970). They kidnapped a British diplomat, James Cross, and a Quebec cabinet minister, Pierre Laporte. At the height of the conflict, Pierre Laporte was murdered.

Conversely, the PQ used democratic methods. In 1976, the PQ, led by René Lévesque won the election, and in 1980, a referendum on sovereignty association was held. The results showed close to 60 percent chose federalism (remaining a part of Canada). In 1995, a second referendum on a similar question produced a difference of only 1 percent in favour of the federalist side.

The Relationship Between English Canada and Quebec

- **Bilingual:** A person or place that uses two languages.
- **Multiculturalism**: A policy of promoting cultural retention rather than assimilation.
- **Anglophones**: English speakers.
- **Repatriate:** To restore or return to the country of origin, allegiance, or citizenship. As used in Canadian history: To bring under Canadian rather than British control.
- **Patriate/Patriation**: A term based on repatriation but used in Canada to mean "to make something part of one's own nation" since repatriation did not really apply.
- **National unity:** A state of harmony between English and French Canada.

After the emergence of Quebec nationalism, the federal government started to make efforts to satisfy the demands of Quebec. In the 1960s, the Royal Commission on Bilingualism and Biculturalism led to the Official Languages Act of 1969, making Canada officially bilingual. Quebec did not feel that national bilingualism was enough to protect its language, so in 1977 the provincial government introduced Bill 101, which was designed to make French the only official language of Quebec. This bill angered Anglophones and immigrants in Quebec who could not speak French. Tensions between federalists and separatists continued.

Prime Minister Pierre Elliot Trudeau's attempts to patriate Canada's constitution came to fruition in 1981; however, Quebec was not a signatory. Under Prime Minister Brian Mulroney, two efforts to have Quebec sign the constitution were made. Both the Meech Lake accord (1990) and the Charlottetown accord (1992) failed to bring about the national unity that federalists so desperately wanted.

1.2.4   identify the major groups of French Canadians outside Quebec and describe some of their efforts to achieve recognition

FRENCH CANADIANS OUTSIDE OF QUEBEC

New Brunswick, Ontario, Manitoba, Alberta, and other areas of Canada have significant populations of Franco-Canadians. The preservation of French-Canadian culture is the focus of a variety of organizations, such as the *Association Canadienne-Francaise d'Education de l'Ontario*, that have fought for French schools in Ontario. Changing their name to the *Association Canadienne-Francaise de Ontario (ACFO)* in 1968, they now focus on other areas as well such as culture, politics, health, community service, and the legal system.

CANADA'S PARTICIPATION IN WAR, PEACE, AND SECURITY

1.3.1   identify the causes of World War I and World War II and explain how Canada became involved in these two wars

CAUSES OF WORLD WAR I AND WORLD WAR II

- **Fascist:** A government based on dictatorship and strong nationalism.
- **Imperialism:** The expansion of one nation's authority over other lands using economic, political, and/or military means.
- **Nationalism:** A strong sense of national pride, often strengthened by imperialism.
- **Militarism:** The build-up of military forces for defensive and offensive political desires.
- **Alliance system**: In Europe, alliances among countries were set up to help maintain peace; ironically, these alliances ensured that most of the countries in Europe were drawn into the war.

In the early 1900s, tensions were running high across Europe because of imperialism, nationalism, militarism, and the alliance system. It was in the Balkans, known as the "powder keg of Europe," where events occurred that activated the alliance system, bringing Germany, Austria-Hungary, and Italy (known as the Triple Alliance) into wars against Britain, France, and Russia (known as the Triple Entente). Britain declared war on Germany on August 4, 1914. This meant Canada, as part of the British Empire, was automatically at war as well.

World War I ended with the Treaty of Versailles, which imposed harsh restrictions on Germany, in the hopes of preventing the German nation from rising up again. World War II was caused in large part by the treaty, because it had created resentment in the German people; this resentment was exploited by German Chancellor Adolf Hitler and his Nazi party to further their own ambitions and goals. In the 1930s, Germany became a fascist country with a desire to correct the perceived injustices of the Treaty of Versailles.

Canada, now a completely sovereign nation, recalled parliament and held an emergency debate and vote regarding World War II. In a nearly unanimous decision, the parliament of Canada made its own declaration of war against Germany approximately one week after Britain.

1.3.2   describe some of the contributions Canada and Canadians made to the war effort overseas during World War I and World War II

CANADA'S CONTRIBUTION TO THE WAR EFFORT OVERSEAS

- **Vimy Ridge"** A strategic ridge in northeast France that gave the Germans a clear view of the battle-field below.
- **D-Day:** The successful landing of 130 000 Allied troops in Normandy, France that opened up the western European theatre of war on June 6, 1944.

Canadians served with distinction and honour in both World Wars I and II. The Battle of Vimy Ridge in April 1917 near the end of World War I was led by Canadian born Major-General Arthur Currie. Vimy Ridge was a major Canadian victory over Germany, despite over 10 000 Canadians being killed or wounded. Canadians also distinguished themselves at Ypres and Passchendaele.

In 1941, Canadian troops fought valiantly to try to keep the strategic location of Hong Kong out of Japanese hands, suffering almost 800 casualties, and losing 257 troops in Japanese prisoner of war (POW) camps. In August 1942, Canadian soldiers took the lead in a failed effort to open up the western front at the French port of Dieppe. Fifteen thousand Canadians were involved in the successful invasion, known as D-Day, that pushed back German forces on the French coast in 1944.

Many Canadians distinguished themselves as heroes in the world wars; two such examples are flying ace Billy Bishop in World War I and Aboriginal Canadian Tommy Prince in World War II.

1.3.3   describe some of the contributions Canada and Canadians made to the war effort at home during World War I and World War II, as well as some of the effects the wars had on the home front

CANADA'S CONTRIBUTION TO THE WAR EFFORT AT HOME

• **Munitions industry:** People or companies in the business of making weapons.

During both world wars, women became important in many aspects of society, including the work force and the military. Because so many men were enlisted and away from their homes and jobs, women stepped in to fill those roles. In World War I, over 30 000 women worked in the munitions industry, and by 1943 well over 200 000 women were working to produce war goods. Women served as nurses during both wars, and in World War II tens of thousands of women signed up to the newly formed Canadian military divisions for women, including the Canadian Women's Auxiliary Air Force (CWAAF), the Canadian Women's Army Corp (CWAC), and the Women's Royal Canadian Naval Service (WRCNS/WRENS).

On December 6, 1917, a French munitions ship collided with a Belgian relief vessel in the Halifax harbour, killing 2 000 people and injuring over 9 000 others. The Halifax Explosion could be heard more than 100 km away; though it was an accident, the explosion brought the horrors of war home to Canadians.

Canada was the home of the British Commonwealth Air Training Plan during World War II. Described as the "Aerodrome of Democracy" by American President F.D. Roosevelt, BCATP trained almost 150 000 men for air force duty, including over 70 000 Canadians.

Camp X was a training base for spies and intelligence agents, both men and women, from Canadian, American, and British forces. It was located just outside of Oshawa, Ontario.

Over 600 000 Canadians served in Canada's Armed Forces during World War I, with nearly 240 000 casualties, including over 60 000 dead. Over 1 million Canadians served in World War II. The casualties included more than 45 000 dead or missing.

1.3.4   describe the events leading up to the Holocaust and assess Canada's response to those events

THE HOLOCAUST AND CANADA'S RESPONSE

• **Holocaust:** The genocide of European Jews and others during World War II.
• **Fascism:** A political philosophy, movement, or régime that holds the nation (and often race) above the individual. Fascist régimes are characterized by a centralized government headed by a dictatorial leader, strict economic and social controls, and repression of opposition.
• **Nazis:** Members of a German fascist party controlling Germany from 1933 to 1945 under Adolf Hitler.
  ▪ Where did the word come from? It is short for the party name *Nationalsozialist,* which comes from *national* (national) + *Sozialist* (socialist).
• **Pogrom**: An organized persecution or massacre of helpless people, such as the Jews.
• **Concentration camps:** A camp where prisoners of war, political prisoners, refugees, or peoples the state considers undesirable are imprisoned.

The Holocaust grew in Germany following the rise to power in 1933 of Adolf Hitler and the Nazis. Hitler became popular and gained power by promising to improve the poor economic situation in Germany, which was blamed on the Treaty of Versailles at the end of World War I and on other peoples (Jews, Poles, Czechs, and Russians) that Hitler thought were inferior to the "true" German race. Germany took away Jewish citizenship rights with the Nuremberg Laws of 1935. Responding to the assassination of a minor Nazi official, the German government authorized a two-day pogrom against Jews in November 1938 referred to as *Kristallnacht.*

Canada did have its own fascist organizations and people who supported the Nazi party. There was also discrimination against Jews across Canada at this time. These groups often clashed with other Canadian groups who did not believe in fascism. Despite evidence of Jews being placed in ghettos and concentration camps, Canada did not offer refuge to Jews in the 1930s.

1.3.5   summarize Canada's role in some key Cold War activities from 1945 to 1989

CANADA AND THE COLD WAR TO 1989

- **Cold War:** Tensions and hostilities between the former Soviet Union and its allies and the United States and its allies.
- **NATO:** North Atlantic Treaty Organization. An alliance of 26 countries from North America and Europe whose members agree to come to one another's defence if attacked by a non-member state.
- **NORAD:** North American Aerospace Defense Command. A bi-national U.S. and Canadian organization charged with the missions of aerospace warning and aerospace control for North America.
- **Espionage:** Spying on the enemy.
- **Asylum:** A type of protection given to refugees by a foreign government.
- **Nuclear arms race:** A competition between or among countries to accumulate the most nuclear weapons.

Canada played an important role in the Cold War. Canada became a committed member of the North Atlantic Treaty Organization (NATO) when it was created in 1949. Canadians joined United Nations forces in 1950 to help repel communist North Korea's attack on non-communist South Korea.

During this time period, Canada was revamping its foreign policy, trying to create a truly Canadian place in world affairs instead of just following Britain and/or the United States. Canada tried to maintain neutrality during the Cuban Missile Crisis by not putting Canada's NORAD aircraft on alert until just before the crisis ended. Canada also did not agree with the Americans about their presence in Vietnam, and Canada allowed "draft dodgers" from the U.S. into Canada and refused to return them to the United States.

Espionage was common during the Cold War. In 1945, Igor Gouzenko was given political asylum in Canada from the U.S.S.R. Another feature of the Cold War was the nuclear arms race between the U.S. and the U.S.S.R.

1.3.6   assess some examples of the roles and functions of the Canadian armed forces since 1945, such as peacekeeping and peacemaking and maintaining security

ROLES AND FUNCTIONS OF THE CANADIAN ARMED FORCES

- **Collective security:** A system for keeping the international peace.

Since World War II, Canada has been a mediator (peacekeeper) in several major crises around the world. Beginning with the Suez Crisis in 1956, and including other peacekeeping and investigation missions in Zaire, Cyprus, Vietnam, Yemen, and Kashmir, Canada has been a part of every UN peacekeeping mission up to 1989.

In the late 1960s, Canada's government began to place less emphasis on foreign relations and defence spending. However, Canada still remained an active member of NATO and NORAD, as well as an active part in Commonwealth aid programs.

PRACTICE QUESTIONS

1. Explain why Medicare and the Canada Health Act are important parts of Canadian identity.

   _____

   _____

   _____

   _____

2. Which of the following statements about Canada's involvement in World War I is **true**?

   A. Canada committed money but not manpower to the war.

   B. When Britain declared war in 1914, Canada was automatically at war.

   C. Canada stayed out of the war because it was strictly a European conflict.

   D. When the United States entered the war in 1917, Canada was automatically at war.

3. Which of the following causes did **not** lead to World War I?

   A. An arms race among the European powers

   B. Ethnic tension in the Austro-Hungarian Empire

   C. Hostilities between Canada and the United States

   D. France's intention to recapture the provinces of Alsace and Lorraine

4. Conscription was controversial during World War I and the governing Conservatives were punished for it in the 1917 election. Explain why, following the introduction of conscription in WWII, the governing Liberals were not punished by Quebec voters in the 1945 election?

   _____

   _____

   _____

   _____

5. Describe an important difference between the Meech Lake accord and the Charlottetown accord.

   _____

   _____

   _____

   _____

6. Which of the following pairs of countries had hostile relations in the early 20th century (early 1900s)?

   A. Russia and Britain

   B. France and Britain

   C. France and Germany

   D. Germany and Austria-Hungary

7. The **best** definition of Camp X is

   A. an air force base during World War II

   B. a training base for intelligence agents

   C. an internment camp for Japanese Canadians

   D. a base where experiments were done using atomic energy

8. Which of the following atrocities did the Japanese commit in Hong Kong during World War II?

   A. Biological weapons were used in battle.

   B. With Nazi assistance, concentration camps for Jews were created.

   C. Non-Japanese Asians were deported to internment camps in mainland China.

   D. A couple hundred Canadian prisoners of war died in prison camps as a result of torture.

9. Give a brief explanation of the Cold War, including the time period and the two major nations involved.

   _____

   _____

   _____

   _____

10. Which of the following statements **best** describes a key difference between Canada and most Western European countries?

    A. Canada's population is more heterogeneous.

    B. Canada's population is more urbanized.

    C. Canada's standard of living is higher.

    D. Canada's standard of living is lower.

11. What is the **most important** purpose of the Canadian Radio-television and Telecommunications Commission?

    _____

    _____

    _____

    _____

12. The Kyoto Protocol is an international agreement that was created to help

    A. reduce tariffs

    B. protect human rights

    C. protect the environment

    D. reduce the number of peacekeeping missions

13. Explain the purpose of NATO and describe how it began.

_____

_____

_____

_____

14. Which of the following sentences about Canada's role in using the atomic bomb during World War II is **true**?

   A. Canadian uranium was used for the atomic bomb.

   B. Canada did not support the use of the atomic bomb.

   C. Canadian pilots flew the fighter planes that dropped the atomic bombs on Japan.

   D. Canada provided no money or material, although they supported the Americans' decision.

15. Which of the following people **most** agreed with conscription in World War I?

   A. Nellie McClung

   B. Wilfred Laurier

   C. Henri Bourassa

   D. Robert Borden

16. Explain **ONE** of the following causes of World War II:

   A. Japanese desires to acquire natural resources

   B. An unsatisfactory resolution to World War I

   C. Adolf Hitler's desire to restore Germany to superpower level

_____

_____

_____

_____

17. What is the **most important** goal of Canada's national defence policy?

_____

_____

_____

_____

18. Explain why Vimy Ridge was an important battle for World War II **AND** why it was an important battle for Canada as a nation.

_____

_____

_____

_____

19. During the 1980s and early 1990s, Quebec's politicians pushed for the recognition of Quebec within Canada's constitution as a

A. distinct society

B. sovereign state

C. bilingual province

D. multicultural nation

20. Which term is used to describe the dramatic transformation of Quebec's cultural and political attitudes during the 1960s?

A. FLQ Crisis

B. Conquest

C. Duplessis Era

D. Quiet Revolution

21. Describe how American culture has affected Canadian lifestyles and culture. State and explain at least one example of how the Canadian government has tried to keep a Canadian identity.

_____

_____

_____

_____

22. The **most important** ingredient in Canadian nationalism is a shared

A. culture

B. identity

C. territory

D. language

23. Which of the following types of nationalism is **most useful** for preserving national unity in a bilingual, multiracial, and multicultural country such as Canada?

A. Civic nationalism

B. Tribal nationalism

C. Ethnic nationalism

D. Cultural nationalism

24. Explain why the Conscription Crisis of 1917 caused French Canadians to feel conflicted loyalty to Quebec and Canada.

_____

_____

_____

_____

25. The Meech Lake accord and the Charlottetown accord were both unsuccessful attempts to
    A. abolish Canada's Senate
    B. amend Canada's constitution
    C. centralize political power in Canada
    D. provide sovereignty-association for Quebec

26. Which of the following rows pairs an international organization with its main purpose?

	Organization	Main Purpose
A.	NORAD	Protects human rights
B.	NATO	Creates a free trade zone
C.	European Union	Promotes ethnic nationalism
D.	United Nations	Maintains international security

27. During World War II, which of the following military divisions were women **not** allowed to be a part of?
    A. RCAF
    B. CWAC
    C. WRENS
    D. CWAAF

28. Which Canadian Prime Minister was awarded the Nobel Peace Prize in 1957?
    A. Paul Martin
    B. Robert Borden
    C. Lester Pearson
    D. Brian Mulroney

29. Explain how Canada's multicultural society helps contribute to Canadian identity.

_____

_____

_____

_____

30. Describe the roles of the Canadian Armed Forces since the end of World War II, and explain how those roles have affected Canadian identity.

_____

_____

_____

_____

ANSWERS AND SOLUTIONS FOR PRACTICE QUESTIONS

1. OR	7. B	13. OR	19. A	25. B
2. B	8. D	14. A	20. D	26. D
3. C	9. OR	15. D	21. OR	27. A
4. OR	10. A	16. OR	22. B	28. C
5. OR	11. OR	17. OR	23. A	29. OR
6. C	12 C	18. OR	24. OR	30. OR

1. **Open Response**

   Medicare was modelled after the New Democratic Party's plan in Saskatchewan in the 1960s. The Canada Health Act was passed in 1984. Having the provincial and federal governments cover the cost of all necessary medical services is a major component of Canadian identity. Our Medicare system sets us distinctly apart from the United States and shows our belief in social programs.

2. **B**

   When World War I began in 1914, Canada was part of the British Empire. Therefore, when Britain declared war, Canada was automatically at war as its foreign affairs were controlled by Britain.

3. **C**

   The relationship Canada had with the United States at that time was not hostile.

   World War I was caused by tensions in Europe, especially between France and Germany, as well as between Russia and Austria-Hungary.

4. **Open Response**

   In 1945, Liberal cabinet minister Louis St. Laurent's personal popularity in Quebec softened anti-Liberal public opinion. Louis St. Laurent became Liberal leader and prime minister in 1949 following Mackenzie King's retirement. St. Laurent was a very popular and well respected Quebec politician, and his presence did in fact reduce the tensions in Quebec.

5. **Open Response**

   The Meech Lake accord needed approval by all the provincial governments, as well as the federal government, while the Charlottetown accord was to be approved by a national referendum.

   Both the Meech Lake and Charlottetown accords were attempts by Progressive Conservative Prime Minister Brian Mulroney to have Quebec sign the constitution of 1982. The discussions leading to the Charlottetown accord involved more than just the prime minister and the 10 premiers; representatives of women and aboriginal groups were also involved.

6. C

France and Germany had hostile relations in the early 20th century. France wanted revenge for losses to Germany in an 18th century war.

France and Britain signed an agreement of friendship in 1904, and Russia and Britain also reached an understanding in 1907. Germany and Austria-Hungary became official allies in 1878.

7. B

Camp X was a training base near Oshawa, Ontario where spies for the British, American, and Canadian Armed Forces were trained.

8. D

After the Japanese attacked Pearl Harbour, they attacked Hong Kong for strategic reasons. Following a 17-day battle on December 1941, 300 of the 2 000 Canadian troops stationed there were killed, and almost 500 were wounded. When Hong Kong surrendered, the remaining Canadians became prisoners of war; 257 died as a result of torture, starvation, or murder.

9. Open Response

The Cold War refers to the hostilities that developed after World War II between the communist Soviet Union (and its satellite states) and the democratic capitalist countries such as Canada, the United States, and Western Europe.

From the mid-1940s through the early 1990s, the two super-power nations of the United States and the Soviet Union were in a rivalry for supremacy in military and technological advances, including nuclear weapons. Although these two countries had fought for the same side during WWII, they came into conflict over differing ideologies (democracy/capitalism vs. communism) and were involved in several conflicts around the world.

10. A

Canada's population is more heterogeneous, or diverse, than most Western European countries.

Standard of living refers to the ways in which a society is able to satisfy its wants and desires as well as its basic needs. The term urbanization refers to the population that is living within a city.

11. Open Response

The most important role of the Canadian Radio-television and Telecommunications Commission is to promote the development of Canadian music and television.

One of the goals of the CRTC is to ensure that at least 50 percent of prime-time programming has Canadian content. It does regulate foreign broadcast content during prime time, but does not prevent it.

12. C

The Kyoto Protocol is a 1997 agreement designed to reduce greenhouse gas emissions worldwide.

13. Open Response

NATO (North Atlantic Treaty Organization) is a military organization that was created in 1949. Canadian diplomats proposed the alliance as a way to support the United States, within a consultation framework, and to keep the Soviet Union from attempting to take over Western Europe. NATO is an organization created for the mutual defence of its members.

14. A

The Canadian government purchased a uranium mine in the Northwest Territories. Canada had the only uranium refinery outside Nazi-occupied Europe at Port Hope, Ontario.

15. D

Conservative Prime Minister Robert Borden favoured compulsory military service. He believed that Canada's participation in the war was the only way Canada would be considered an equal to Great Britain.

Liberal opposition leader Wilfrid Laurier opposed conscription; however, he was less aggressive in his opposition than Henri Bourassa who was a publisher of *Le Devoir*, an influential French Canadian newspaper. Nellie McClung opposed conscription and going to war.

16. Open Response

A. The Japanese wanted to acquire natural resources, which brought them into conflict with the United States, Britain, China, Western allies, and other South Pacific countries. Japan's actions brought about embargoes against them and eventually led to the United States declaring war on Japan.

B. The Treaty of Versailles ended World War I, and it contained harsh penalties and restrictions on Germany in order to keep Germany from gaining power.

C. The German people suffered because of the Treaty, so Hitler was able to use this suffering, and his promises for change and retribution, to gain popularity and control in Germany. Hitler's rise to power, and his actions within Europe, led to World War II.

17. Open Response

The top priority of Canada's (and any nation's) national defence policy is national security; that is, keeping members of the nation free from danger, harm, or threat. There are other goals such as providing peacekeepers for UN missions, pushing for the enlargement of the NATO alliance, and disposing of landmines in war-torn areas of the globe.

18. Open Response

The Battle of Vimy Ridge created a much stronger Canadian nationalism, which eventually led to Canadian sovereignty.

Historians claim that Canada became a nation on the day that Canadian soldiers captured Vimy Ridge. What they mean by this is that Canadians first developed a strong national pride as a result of their spectacular achievement. The stronger nationalism that emerged after the battle made Canadians more determined to end Canada's status as a mere colony of Great Britain. Canadians achieved this goal in 1931—only 14 years after the Battle of Vimy Ridge. Canadian nationalism—albeit a relatively weak nationalism—existed prior to the battle. Canadians had taken other significant steps toward sovereignty before 1918 (Confederation in 1867, for instance). The battle did a lot to create a Canadian national consciousness.

19. A

Liberal governments in Quebec in the 1980s and 1990s pushed for recognition of Quebec as a "distinct society"—especially in the Meech Lake and Charlottetown accords. Although Parti Québécois governments have pushed for Quebec sovereignty, they have never pursued recognition of Quebec's independence in the Canadian constitution. After all, no nation's constitution recognizes the sovereignty of another sovereign country. Quebec separatists ultimately wanted to create a new constitution for an independent Quebec. In the 1980s and 1990s, virtually all provincial politicians in Quebec opposed the policies of bilingualism and multiculturalism. They pursued policies of unilingualism within Quebec and preferred the old model of biculturalism over the new model of multiculturalism.

20. D

The Quiet Revolution was the Lesage era of the 1960s during which Quebec rapidly modernized. The dramatic transformation of Quebec's culture, government, and society during this time is known as the Quiet Revolution. It was, in part, a rebellion against the ultraconservative economic, social, and political systems established and maintained by Duplessis.

The Conquest refers to the British use of military force to overcome and control New France (Quebec) from 1759 to 1760. Through the conquest, Quebec ceased to be a colony of France and became a British colony. The FLQ Crisis (October Crisis) occurred in Quebec in 1970. It was a struggle between the government and Québécois separatist terrorists from the *Front de libération du Québec* (FLQ). The Duplessis Era refers to the tenure of Quebec's authoritarian provincial premier Maurice Duplessis, who was in power in Quebec during most of the 1936 to 1959 period.

21. Open Response

Canadians are greatly affected by American culture. From advertising to books, and from television to movies, American culture is constantly influencing Canadians.

The Canadian government created the CTRC to help maintain Canadian content in Canadian radio and television programming. The Canadian Broadcasting Company (CBC) and the National Film Board (NFB) were also created to help create and highlight Canadian culture.

22. B

A shared group identity is the basis of nationalism and nationhood. Nationalism exists whenever a group views itself as a nation. Nationalism can exist when a group shares a common identity, but does not share a common culture, territory, or language.

Shared culture, territory, or language is less important in maintaining nationalism than a shared group identity. There are plenty of examples of nations that have lost their culture, territory, or language but continue to share a national identity; for example, the Jewish, Irish, or Palestinian nations.

23. A

Civic nationalism binds people together through a shared belief in the same laws, values, and political traditions. It is capable of uniting people who do not share the same race, ethnicity, culture, or language.

The terms "tribal nationalism" and "cultural nationalism" are synonymous with the term "ethnic nationalism." These nationalisms are only useful for uniting individuals who share the same ancestry or cultural traditions. Consequently, they would not be effective instruments for unifying Canada's linguistically and culturally diverse population.

24. Open Response

During the Conscription Crisis of 1917, French Canadians experienced great conflict between their loyalties to Quebec and Canada. Many French Canadians resented being forced to fight in a war they believed to be Britain's fight, not Canada's, and certainly not Quebec's.

25. B

The Meech Lake accord (1990) and the Charlottetown accord (1992) were unsuccessful attempts to amend (change) Canada's constitution. Their primary goal was to accommodate Quebec, which had refused to approve the 1982 constitutional deal brokered by Prime Minister Pierre Trudeau.

Neither accord attempted to abolish the Senate (although the Charlottetown accord sought to reform it) or to award Quebec sovereignty-association (national independence for Quebec, but with close economic ties to the rest of Canada). Both accords sought to decentralize the Canadian federation (grant more power to the provinces) rather than to centralize the federation (concentrate more power in the hands of the federal government).

26. D

One of the main goals of the UN is to maintain world peace through collective security.

NORAD (North American Aerospace Defense Command) is a military alliance, not a human rights protection organization. NATO (North Atlantic Treaty Organization) is a military alliance. The European Union is an organization that strives for the economic and political integration of Europe by promoting international cooperation and a multicultural European civic nationalism. Promoting ethnic nationalism (a force that tends to divide Europeans rather than unite them) is certainly not the main goal of the EU.

27. A

RCAF—Royal Canadian Air Force: Women were **not** allowed to serve with this unit during World War II.

WRENS—Women's Royal Canadian Naval Service: Established in 1942, and by 1945, 7 100 women had signed up.

CWAC—Canadian Women's Army Corps: Established in 1941, and by 1945 21 500 women had joined.

CWAAF—Canadian Women's Auxiliary Air Force: Established in 1941, and by 1945 17 400 women had served.

28. C

Lester B. Pearson was awarded the Nobel Peace Prize in 1957 for his work in brokering a peace agreement in the Suez Crisis. Pearson was Canada's acting minister of external affairs at the time of the crisis, and he suggested that the UN send in a peacekeeping contingent while a settlement was being worked out. The peacekeeping units stopped the fighting and restored peace to the region; this effort marked the beginning of UN peacekeeping missions, with Canada as a major leader and contributor to those missions ever since.

29. Open Response

Because the people of Canada have so many different cultures, religions, languages, etc., Canada's society is often described as a "mosaic." While these differences can sometimes cause conflict, it is just this cultural mosaic and general acceptance that makes our Canadian identity unique.

30. Open Response

Since the end of World War II, the Canadian Armed Forces have distinguished themselves as peacekeepers and peacemakers and have also been active members in humanitarian aid programs. Canada maintains an active role in both NATO and UN missions, providing troops, funding, and aid to regions around the world in need.

These roles on the world stage often help create a feeling of Canadian identity because these efforts have meant Canadians are well-respected by other countries.

UNIT TEST

Use the following information to answer the next question.

Speaker I	I believe that Canada is a nation based on the ideas of the British Common Law. There should not be any doubt that first and foremost we are descendants of the British, and we should pursue British immigrants.
Speaker II	This country is made up of many different ethnic groups. An immigration policy that takes in people from everywhere is an important part of what defines Canada. We are a mosaic, not a melting pot.
Speaker III	I feel that the immigrants who make the best Canadians are ones who do not stand out.
Speaker IV	While I believe in open immigration, there are some immigrants who do not fit in, and we need to be careful that we do not accept too many immigrants from certain cultures.

1. Which speaker seems to **most** agree with Canada's multicultural policies?

    A. Speaker I

    B. Speaker II

    C. Speaker III

    D. Speaker IV

2. Which of the following roles is indicative of Canada's participation in international events since World War II?

    A. Helping in the capture of Vimy Ridge

    B. Sending peacekeepers to the Middle East

    C. Being a member of the League of Nations

    D. Accepting foreign aid to deal with poverty

3. State the time periods and give a brief description of **TWO** missions that Canadian troops were involved in since World War II as a part of Canada's commitment to the United Nations.

    _____

    _____

    _____

    _____

Use the following fictional news article to answer the next question.

In his last few years as prime minister, he was not very popular. In addition to implementing policies that seemed to alienate Western Canada, he failed to have Quebec join the constitutional family.

4. Which Canadian prime minister does the fictional news article refer to?

　　A. Paul Martin

　　B. Jean Chrétien

　　C. Pierre Trudeau

　　D. Brian Mulroney

Use the following fictional newspaper story to answer the next question.

(Fictionally published in January 1992)

In November 1989, the Berlin Wall, separating East and West Germany, came down without opposition from the Soviet Union. It became apparent that the Cold War was coming to an end, and now the Soviet Union itself ceases to exist. Russia, the largest Republic of the former U.S.S.R., is working toward becoming a democratic country with a market economy. President Boris Yeltsin and U.S. President George Bush have held several discussions about how the United States and other Western countries can help Russia's transformation.

5. Given the above information, state your opinion on the following question: "Should Canadians continue to spend money on NATO commitments?"

_____

_____

_____

_____

6. Explain why French Canadians did not want to fight in World War I.

_____

_____

_____

_____

7. Which of the following statements about the two referenda held in Quebec is **true**?

　　A. René Lévesque was the premier during both votes.

　　B. The Parti Québécois opposed sovereignty association.

　　C. More people supported sovereignty association in 1980 than in 1995.

　　D. In 1995, the difference in "yes" and "no" votes was approximately 1 percent.

8. Which bill regarding language issues did René Lévesque pass while he was premier? Provide a description of the bill and state its significance for all of Canada.

_____

_____

_____

_____

9. Which of the following results occurred when the provinces failed to ratify the Meech Lake accord by June 30, 1990?

   A. Prime Minister Mulroney resigned.

   B. Preston Manning formed the Reform Party.

   C. Quebec's premier Robert Bourassa resigned.

   D. The Mulroney government made a second effort to get support for a new constitutional package in 1992.

10. Explain how **TWO** of the following causes led to World War I:

   A. Imperialism

   B. Nationalism

   C. Militarism

   D. The Alliance System

11. The Nazis dealt with opposition to their policies by

   A. doing nothing

   B. encouraging discussion

   C. eliminating political opponents

   D. campaigning harder in the next election

12. Briefly describe the Battle of Dieppe and why it was important for the future successes of Allied landings.

_____

_____

_____

_____

Use the following information to answer the next question.

A student working on a report gathered the following factual information:

- The Royal Rifles of Canada and the Winnipeg Grenadiers—the first Canadian ground units to see action in World War II—fought valiantly to defend the colony.
- In all, 290 soldiers were killed and 493 were wounded.
- On December 24, the Japanese overran a makeshift hospital, assaulted and murdered nurses, and bayoneted wounded Canadian soldiers in their beds.
- More than 550 of the 1 975 Canadians who sailed from Vancouver in October 1941 never returned.

13. The **best** title for the student's report is

   A. "Murder of Canadian Prisoners"

   B. "Canada's Role in World War II"

   C. "Nazi Atrocities During World War II"

   D. "Atrocities Committed by the Japanese at Hong Kong"

14. Since 1914, political leaders have created and implemented several policies that have contributed to a sense of Canadian identity. Choose **ONE** of these policies to *describe*, then *state* which politician put it into action, and *explain* how this policy helps create a feeling of Canadian identity.

   A. Canadian Charter of Rights and Freedoms

   B. The Canadian Radio-television and Telecommunications Commission (CRTC)

_____

_____

_____

_____

15. Describe Canada's immigration policy after World War II.

_____

_____

_____

_____

16. The North Atlantic Treaty Organization is **best** described as an agreement with the purpose of

   A. defending against Islamic terrorists

   B. defending against Soviet expansion

   C. promoting trade among its members

   D. working toward reducing air pollution

17. To which of the following collective security organizations has Canada **never** belonged?

    A. Warsaw Pact

    B. United Nations

    C. League of Nations

    D. North Atlantic Treaty Organization

18. In which of the following countries have Canadian troops **not** served as either peacekeepers or peacemakers?

    A. Cuba

    B. Korea

    C. Bosnia

    D. Afghanistan

19. Describe at least **THREE** contributions of Canadian women during both World Wars and how those involvements impacted Canadian culture after the wars ended.

_____

_____

_____

_____

20. Explain why the "Duplessis Years" in Quebec were also known as "The Great Darkness."

_____

_____

_____

ANSWERS AND SOLUTIONS FOR UNIT TEST

1. B	5. OR	9. D	13. D	17. A
2. B	6. OR	10. OR	14. OR	18. A
3. OR	7. D	11. C	15. OR	19. OR
4. D	8. OR	12. OR	16. C	20. OR

1. B

The only speaker that willingly accepts immigrants of any linguistic, ethno-cultural, or religious society is Speaker II.

2. B

Canada has been involved in many peacekeeping missions since World War II, including the Middle East on several different occasions.

Canada did play a large role in capturing Vimy Ridge and did join the League of Nations; however, both of those actions were before World War II. As well, Canada is a giver, not a receiver of foreign aid.

3. Open Response

Canada's first peacekeeping mission was in the Suez Canal Crisis in 1956. This conflict started when Egypt (who was supported by the Soviet Union) took control of the canal from France and Britain. Canadian peacekeeping troops were able to maintain the peace while negotiations took place.

Canadian troops originally went to Bosnia as United Nations peacekeepers among Bosnians, Serbs, and Croats in 1992 and again as peacemakers with NATO in 1995.

Canada has been part of every UN peacekeeping mission since 1956.

4. D

For a variety of reasons, including his government's two failed attempts to have Quebec sign the constitution, Brian Mulroney did in fact leave office in 1993 as one of the least popular prime ministers in Canadian history.

5. Open Response

In early 1992, Canadians were in fact questioning whether or not to reduce military expenditures, and especially if NATO, whose purpose was to fight Soviet expansion, was obsolete.

Participation in the UN is necessary because there are plenty of other trouble spots around the globe. An increase in military spending in case the Cold War were to resume was not a question that generated a lot of discussion.

6. Open Response

The main reason for opposition to conscription in World War I was the French Canadian belief that the war was not a threat to Canadian freedom.

Quebecers believed themselves to be loyal Canadians, and they did not object to fighting on the basis of religion (They were not conscientious objectors.). Western farmers opposed conscription because they needed their young men for farming.

7. D

In 1995, when Jacques Parizeau was premier, the difference between the two sides was around 1 percent.

The Parti Québécois supported sovereignty association. In the first referendum, when René Lévesque was premier, approximately 60 percent of Quebecers voted "no."

8. Open Response

Premier René Lévesque passed Bill 101, essentially banning the use of English in Quebec and, with few exceptions, requiring signs to be in French only.

9. D

When the provinces failed to ratify the Meech Lake accord in 1990, the Mulroney government tried again in 1992. The Charlottetown accord was presented to Canadians for ratification by way of a national referendum. It did not receive enough support.

Neither Mulroney nor Bourassa resigned. Preston Manning created the Reform Party in 1987 to protect western interests.

10. Open Response

Imperialism—The colonization of other countries set up arguments between the European nations that were competing for colonies of economic value.

Nationalism—The feeling of national pride was often strengthened by a country's expanding colonial empire and increasing military presence; this feeling and these actions again led to increased competition and arguments between countries.

Militarism—In order to increase and defend growing empires, countries needed to increase their military. This made other countries uncomfortable, causing them to increase their own militaries.

The Alliance System—Many countries began to form alliances to help maintain their safety; however, these alliances meant that a disagreement between two countries would end up bringing several other countries into the fray because of the alliances involved.

It was a combination of all four of these factors that brought about the beginning of the First World War.

11. C

Nazi Germany was not tolerant of opposition to the government. In addition to making other political parties illegal, the Nazis placed dissenters in concentration camps, which ultimately became death camps during World War II.

12. Open Response

The Battle of Dieppe occurred in August of 1942 when 5 000 Canadian soldiers were sent to attack the strongly defended port. German soldiers were placed on cliffs high above the beaches where the Canadian soldiers were landing. The Germans were able to shoot the soldiers as they ran down the landing ramps, and the few who made it to the beach were shot as they raced for cover. Of the 5 000 Canadians sent to Dieppe, 1 000 died, 500 were wounded, and 2 000 became prisoners of war.

The Battle of Dieppe was important for the future successes of Allied landings because the lessons learned at Dieppe contributed to the success of later Allied landings. Although a disaster at the time, Dieppe was viewed by many as a dress rehearsal for D-Day.

13. D

The best title for the student's essay is "Atrocities Committed by the Japanese at Hong Kong." The four points in the student's report relate to the Canadian attempt to defend the Island of Hong Kong and the fact that they were not only overrun by the Japanese, but were treated brutally in captivity.

14. Open Response

A. Canadian Charter of Rights and Freedoms: In 1982, Prime Minister Pierre Trudeau used this bill to entrench certain political and civil rights into the Canadian Constitution; it applies only to government laws and actions. These rights show what Canadians value as part of our national identity.

B. CRTC: Created in 1968 by Trudeau's Liberal government, the CRTC mandates that radio stations must have 30 percent Canadian content in their programming and television stations must have 60 percent of prime-time productions made in Canada, with no more than 30 percent of programming coming from one country. The rules put in place by the CRTC help ensure that Canadian content will have a place in media.

15. Open Response

Canada opened its doors to refugees from Hungary in 1956. Nearly 5 million immigrants came to Canada between 1946 and 1979. Visible minorities were accepted as immigrants especially in the 1970s when more than half of Canada's immigrants were from Asia or Caribbean nations. Good health and marketable skills were important conditions for coming to Canada.

16. C

NATO's purpose was to defend against Soviet expansion. It was formed in 1949, near the beginning of the Cold War. Its 12 original members included Canada, the United States, and 10 Western European nations.

17. A

Canada was never a member of the Warsaw Pact, which was the Soviet equivalent of NATO and no longer exists.

Canada was a member of the League of Nations between World War I and II. Canada is currently a member of the United Nations and the North Atlantic Treaty Organization.

18. A

Canadian troops have not served as either peacekeepers or peacemakers in Cuba. International conflict related to Cuba occurred in 1961 and 1962, but it was dealt with by the two superpowers of the day: the United States and the Soviet Union.

19. Open Response

During both World Wars, Canadian women were called out of their homes to help with the war effort. Women went to work in the fields and in the factories. Women joined special divisions of the Canadian forces, such as: the Canadian Women's Auxiliary Air Force (CWAAF), the Canadian Women's Army Corp (CWAC), and the Women's Royal Canadian Naval Service (WRCNS/WRENS).

After the wars had ended, Canadian women wanted to maintain the independence they had gained during the wars. Women fought to gain the vote and for equality. The contributions made by women after both World Wars forever changed the dynamic between men and women in Canada.

20. Open Response

The "Duplessis Years" in Quebec were also known as "The Great Darkness" because Premier Maurice Duplessis believed that, to protect the French culture, he needed to maintain the province's language and Roman Catholic faith and shut out the rest of the country and world. Duplessis encouraged English-speaking business people and industries, but the Quebecers who worked in these industries often felt mistreated.

Quebecers wanted social change and began to see Duplessis as old-fashioned. Quebec was becoming a non-religious (secular) society and the people of Quebec wanted to modernize the economy, the government, and education. The call for a more modern Quebec resulted in people referring to the Duplessis era as "the Great Darkness".

Class Focus
Change and Continuity

TABLE OF CORRELATIONS				
Strand	**General Expectation**	**Specific Outcome**	**Practice Questions**	**Unit Test**
2 Change and Continuity	2.1 explain some major ways in which Canada's population has changed since 1914	12.1.1 identify some major groups of immigrants that have come to Canada since 1914 and describe the circumstances that led to their immigration	3, 8	
		2.1.2 describe some of the ways in which Canadian immigration policies have changed over time and how such changes have affected patterns of immigration	1, 9	1, 3
		2.1.3 explain some of the ways in which the lives of adolescents, women, and seniors have changed since World War I as a result of major demographic shifts and social changes		4
		2.1.4 describe the changing impact of the baby boom generation on Canadian society from the 1950's to the present	4, 10	5, 6
	2.2 evaluate the impact of some technological developments on Canadians in different periods	2.2.1 explain how some key technological developments have changed the everyday lives of Canadians since World War I	5, 11, 20	7, 14
		2.2.2 explain how some key technological innovations in military and other fields have changed the way war has been planned and fought, and describe their impact on combatants and civilians		15
		2.2.3 describe the effects of selected scientific and technological innovations developed by Canadi	12, 13	8

2.3 describe changes in Canada's international status and its role in the world since 1914	2.3.1 identify changes in Canada's international status since World War I	6, 7, 14	9, 10
	2.3.2 describe Canada's responses to some of the major human tragedies that have occurred since World War I	15, 18	2, 11, 12
	2.3.3 describe the development of Canada's role as a world leader in defending human rights since World War II	16, 17	13
	2.3.4 summarize Canada's changing relationship with the United States	2, 19	

CHANGE AND CONTINUITY

DEMOGRAPHIC PATTERNS

2.1.1 identify some major groups of immigrants that have come to Canada since 1914 and describe the circumstances that led to their immigration

IMMIGRATION TO CANADA

- **Immigrants:** People who settle in a country they were not born in.
- **Intolerance:** A lack of acceptance.
- **Refugees:** People who have left their home country to seek safety in another country.
- **Anti-semitism:** Hatred and discrimination against Jews.
- **Displaced persons:** People forced out of their homeland by war.
- **Ethnic origin:** The cultural, racial, and linguistic background of a person.
- **Boat people:** People who seek refugee status by leaving their home country by boat, often in an unsafe vessel. A term that came into use after Vietnamese refugees fled after the Vietnam War.

The nation of Canada is made up of immigrants. After World War I, many immigrants came to Canada in search of peace and a new, prosperous life. Most of these immigrants were European. Immigration from Asia was discouraged and European immigrants whose first language was not English were greeted with intolerance and prejudice.

Because of the high unemployment rate in Canada during the Depression of the 1930s, immigration was very limited. Only 4 000 Jewish refugees fleeing German anti-Semitism were taken in by Canada, a dismal amount when compared to the numbers of Jewish immigrants that Britain and the United States welcomed.

Canada accepted many displaced persons after World War II; however, people were still denied access to Canada based on nationality and ethnicity. As the decades passed, Canadian immigration policies changed. Many people sought refuge in Canada, trying to escape injustices and wars in their home countries. Some people abused the refugee status entry system (by jumping the queue), so Canada needed to find a system that would help legitimate refugees and still use the proper immigration channels.

2.1.2   describe some of the ways in which Canadian immigration policies have changed over time, and how such changes have affected patterns of immigration

CURRENT AND HISTORICAL PATTERNS OF IMMIGRATION TO CANADA

- **Closed door policy:** A Canadian policy that did not allow immigrants from certain countries.
- **Emigrants:** People who leave their country.
- **Racism:** Discrimination based on colour, race, religion, or culture.

The Canadian government has had a variety of policies regarding immigration. In the early 1900s, settling the West was a priority, so Immigration Minister Clifford Sifton promised free land to Eastern Europeans, in particular, Slavs, Hungarians, and Russians. Canada had a closed door policy toward Asians, Africans, and Jews during this time. After World War I, more immigrants were allowed into Canada; however, during the Depression, there were actually more emigrants *from* Canada than immigrants *to* Canada.

After World War II and up until the early 1960s, a vast majority of immigrants to Canada were displaced Europeans. The Immigration Act of 1952 barred people from entering Canada.

This policy changed in 1962 when immigrants were accepted based on Canada's occupational needs, not on their nationality. By the late 1970s, Canada was accepting boat people as well as significant numbers of non-European immigrants and refugees.

In 1978, a new immigration act had three goals: promoting family reunion, upholding humanitarian values, and encouraging economic growth in Canada. Because of this new policy, Canada not only accepted more refugees from Asia, Africa, and South America but also a large number of persons of colour, which reflected a "zero tolerance" policy for racism.

2.1.3   explain some of the ways in which the lives of adolescents, women, and seniors have changed since World War I as a result of major demographic shifts and social changes

URBANIZATION AND POPULATION SHIFTS

- **Rural:** Of or relating to areas of sparse population, usually considered countryside or farmland.
- **Urban:** Of or relating to cities.
- **Suburbs:** Outlying areas of cities.

After World War I, farming became more mechanized, so fewer workers were needed in rural settings. These workers then moved into towns and cities looking for work and opportunities in urban industry.

After World War II, as more Canadians drove cars and public transit increased, the population began to shift out of cities and into planned communities called suburbs. More women entered the workforce, and the increased numbers of children and teenagers (because of the baby boom) caused companies to change the way they marketed their products. All of these factors contributed to a changing economy and to changing lifestyles.

2.1.4   describe the changing impact of the baby boom generation on Canadian society from the 1950s to the present

THE BABY BOOM GENERATION

- **Demographers**: People who study population trends.
- **Pension**: A government plan is paid into by the government and working people and will pay out money for retirement. A private plan is paid into by an employee and his/her employer and will pay out money for retirement.

After the end of World War II, there was a population explosion until the 1960s. This time period is known as "the baby boom." The war was over and the economy was doing well, so more young couples than ever decided to get married and start families. This generation forced Canada to become a "youth-centred society," meaning more schools needed to be built, more teachers had to be hired, and society in general began to change to meet the needs of this large population of young people.

In the 1970s and 1980s, "the boomers" married and started families (their children are known as Generation X and Generation Y), increasing the demand for housing, which led to large price increases. Today, in the 21st century, demographers recognize that as the large population of baby boomers age and retire, Canada's pension plans and health-care systems will be severely challenged.

IMPACT OF SCIENTIFIC AND TECHNOLOGICAL DEVELOPMENTS

By the end of this course, students will:

2.2.1   explain how some key technological developments have changed the everyday lives of Canadians since World War I

TECHNOLOGICAL DEVELOPMENTS AND THE LIVES OF CANADIANS

- **Industrialized world**: The more economically developed countries.
- **Biotechnology:** The use of living organisms to make new drugs and other medical products.

New technology in the industrialized world throughout the 20th, and now 21st, century has had both a positive and negative effect on Canadians. Technology has changed the way people live dramatically.

Communication keeps getting faster and faster, through smaller and smaller devices; from radio and television, to the telephone, to the cell phone and the Internet, people are able to communicate instantaneously with others thousands of miles away. When computers were first invented, they took up several floors in a building. Today, people can take a picture, surf the Internet, and call or text a friend with a single handheld device. Ironically, this technology that was supposed to make our lives easier and more connected has in some ways ended up making our lives busier, more hectic, and less connected personally.

Biotechnology and advances in medicine have given people longer life expectancies.

2.2.2 explain how some key technological innovations in military and other fields have changed the way war has been planned and fought, and describe their impact on combatants and civilians

TECHNOLOGICAL INNOVATIONS

• **Delivery systems:** Methods of getting weapons to their target.

Prior to World War I, wars were fought by men in hand-to-hand combat. The Industrial Revolution saw many inventions that were developed or adapted for military use. Chemical weapons were used during World War I, and many countries have continued to develop and/or use chemical weapons, despite several attempts in history to ban their use. Many new technologies were used in both world wars, including nuclear arms and aircraft, making war deadlier than ever.

These new technologies often mean that there is less hand-to-hand combat, as missiles and bombs are deployed from miles away, sometimes from another country. This style of combat also makes civilian casualties more likely. Some people believe that this less personal, hands-off style of warfare makes it easier to forget the human lives and societies that are destroyed.

2.2.3 describe the effects of selected scientific and technological innovations developed by Canadians

TECHNOLOGICAL INNOVATIONS OF CANADIAN SCIENTISTS

• **Innovations:** New things or methods.

• **Canadarm;** A device used by space shuttles to manipulate objects in space by remote control.

Canadians have made some important innovations. In 1929, Elsie Gregory MacGill became the first woman to receive an electrical engineering degree from the University of Toronto, and during World War II, she was the head of production for the Hawker Hurricane fighter plane. In 1926, Edward Rogers invented the first radio to work on household electricity, and in 1937, Joseph-Armand Bombardier invented the first snowmobile.

In the late 1950s, one of the fastest and most sophisticated fighter planes of the times, the Avro Arrow, was developed in Canada. The controversial cancellation of this project led to lost jobs, and many talented Canadian scientists and engineers moved to the United States to work. In the 1980s, the Canadarm was designed in Quebec.

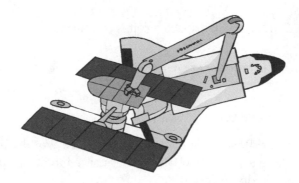

CANADA'S INTERNATIONAL POSITION

2.3.1   identify changes in Canada's international status since World War I

THE EVOLUTION OF CANADIAN POLITICAL AUTONOMY

- **Amend:** To change.
- **Constitution**: The basic set of laws of Canada.
- **Treaty of Versailles:** The peace treaty formally ending World War I.
- **Autonomy:** Total self-government.
- **Repatriate:** To restore or return to the country of origin, allegiance, or citizenship. As used in Canadian history: To bring under Canadian rather than British control.

When the Dominion of Canada was created in 1867, only Britain had the power to amend the Canadian Constitution. Canada's performance in World War I led to the Canadian government receiving its own seat at the Paris Peace Conference in 1919, which created the Treaty of Versailles. At the 1926 Imperial Conference, the Balfour Report accepted the fact that the dominions in the British Empire were autonomous, and in 1931, the British Parliament enacted the Statute of Westminster, giving Canada autonomy and equal status with Britain within the British Commonwealth. Despite this, it took until 1982 for Canada to repatriate the constitution, which was not without controversy.

Canada's Contribution to International Organizations

Canada has made contributions to many organizations that try to make the world a better place. In 1948, a Canadian named John Humphrey wrote the Universal Declaration of Human Rights, which was signed by all 48 members of the United Nations, including Canada. The goal of this declaration is to ensure freedom, equality, and protection under the law to all people.

Canadians have contributed to all UN peacekeeping missions worldwide since the inception of UN peacekeeping missions. In 1968, the government created the Canadian International Development Agency (CIDA) to provide direct assistance to developing countries.

In the 1990s, Canada signed the Convention on the Rights of the Child, a United Nations agreement to work toward protecting the rights of those under 18. Canadians are also involved in the International Campaign to Ban Landmines.

All of these contributions have led to the much respected status of Canadians in the eyes of other countries.

2.3.2   describe Canada's responses to some of the major human tragedies that have occurred since World War I

CANADA'S RESPONSE TO TRAGEDIES SINCE WORLD WAR I

Canada has had various responses to different manmade tragedies since World War I. The genocide in Ukraine from 1932 to 1933, when at least 3 million Ukrainians starved to death, and the Holocaust during World War II, are examples of Canada doing very little.

On the other hand, in the 1990s, in the African nation of Somalia, which faced both civil war and famine, Canada did send 845 troops to help; however, this mission became controversial as Canadian soldiers were involved in the torture and death of a young Somali. Canadians also served in Bosnia in the 1990s as part of a UN peacekeeping force and again as part of a North Atlantic Treaty Organization (NATO) force that came in 1995 to keep peace.

Following the September 11, 2001 terrorist attacks on the United States, Canadian troops joined the UN coalition in Afghanistan to force out the supporters of al-Qaeda, the group responsible for the attack.

2.3.3   describe the development of Canada's role as a world leader in defending human rights since World War II

CANADA'S DEFENCE OF HUMAN RIGHTS SINCE WORLD WAR II

Canadians have been strong defenders of human rights internationally. When the United Nation's Universal Declaration of Human Rights was written in 1948, John Humphrey, a Montreal law professor, was involved. The Ontario Human Rights Code, created in 1962, was the first of its kind in Canada, and the Ontario Human Rights Commission was empowered to investigate complaints and award settlements in cases of human rights violations in that province. Canada's Human Rights Act (1977) gave Canadians the right to examine any government files kept on them, and the Charter of Rights and Freedoms (1982) was entrenched (written into; therefore, difficult to remove) in the constitution.

In the 1990s, Canadian Louise Arbour worked as the chief UN prosecutor for war crimes and human rights abuses in Rwanda and the former Yugoslavia.

2.3.4   summarize Canada's changing relationship with the United States

CANADA'S CHANGING RELATIONSHIP WITH THE UNITED STATES

• **Subsidizing:** Giving financial assistance.

The relationship between Canada and the United States has changed over the years. Before the U.S. began to fight in World War II, they supported Canada and the other Allies with the Lend-Lease Act, which gave war materials to the Allies to be paid for later. Another example of cooperation was when Canada and the United States collaborated with each other in the 1950s to build the St. Lawrence Seaway, linking the Great Lakes to the Atlantic Ocean via the St. Lawrence River.

On occasion, Canada's policies have conflicted with those of the United States. During the Vietnam War of the 1960s, Canada was a safe place for American draft resisters to come. The voyage of the *Manhattan*, an American oil tanker, in 1969 was a challenge to Canada's sovereignty over coastal waters of the Arctic Ocean. In 1974, Canada created the Foreign Investment Review Agency (FIRA) to ensure that foreign (mostly American) takeover of Canadian firms was in the best interests of the Canadian economy. The United States and Canada have also disagreed about softwood lumber, with the U.S. claiming that both the British Columbia government and the federal government were unfairly subsidizing the Canadian lumber industry. Another conflict occurred when the United States led a coalition to invade Iraq in 2003; Canada chose not to take part because the invasion was not approved by the United Nations.

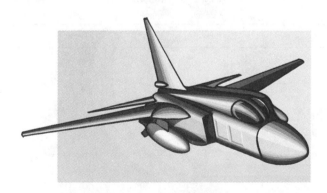

PRACTICE QUESTIONS

1. Describe Canada's immigration policies and the reasons for those policies prior to World War II.

   _____

   _____

   _____

   _____

   _____

   _____

2. State the purpose of the Canada-U.S. Free Trade Agreement of 1989.

   _____

   _____

   _____

   _____

   _____

   _____

3. Which of the following people is **most** associated with bringing immigrants to Canada in the early part of the 20th century?
   A. Clifford Sifton

   B. Robert Borden

   C. Wilfrid Laurier

   D. Mackenzie King

4. Explain the reason for the growth of suburbs after World War II.

   _____

   _____

   _____

   _____

   _____

Use the following information to answer the next question.

Nuclear power meets more than 50% of Ontario's electricity needs. It has two major benefits—low operating costs and virtually none of the emissions that lead to smog, acid rain, or global warming. These benefits make nuclear power a very attractive option for meeting the province's electricity needs well into the future. In the four decades that nuclear energy has served Canada's energy needs, no member of the public has ever been harmed as a result of radiation emission from a nuclear power plant or waste storage facility.

5. Some people are reluctant to support the construction of nuclear power stations because nuclear power
    A. has a lot of emissions
    B. is an expensive form of energy
    C. has been around a very short time
    D. is associated with nuclear weapons

6. Describe the Balfour Report of 1926 in regards to Britain and Canada.

    _____
    _____
    _____
    _____
    _____
    _____

7. Canada does **not** belong to which of the following international organizations?
    A. The United Nations
    B. The European Union
    C. The Commonwealth
    D. La Francophonie

8. State one of the reasons for a large increase in immigration to Canada in the 15-year period following World War II.

    _____
    _____
    _____
    _____
    _____
    _____

9. New regulations were added to the Immigration Act in 1962 in order to

   A. keep out certain ethnic groups

   B. discourage visible minorities

   C. bring in people based on their skills

   D. accept people based only on their income levels

10. Describe some of the problems that are expected for the near future because of the baby boom that followed World War II.

    _____

    _____

    _____

    _____

    _____

    _____

11. Which of the following results of new technology is **least likely**?

    A. Lower prices

    B. A lower standard of living

    C. Rapid depletion of resources

    D. A loss of certain types of jobs

12. Many Canadian women have made huge contributions to society. Describe Elsie Gregory MacGill's contribution to science and technology.

    _____

    _____

    _____

    _____

    _____

13. Explain what happened with the Avro Arrow fighter jet project of the 1950s.

    _____

    _____

    _____

    _____

    _____

14. Which of the following documents gave Canada total legal sovereignty?

    A. War Measures Act

    B. Treaty of Versailles

    C. Statute of Westminster

    D. British North America Act

15. List at least two of Canada's roles in the United Nations.

_____

_____

_____

_____

_____

_____

16. Which of the following Canadians was involved in drawing up the Universal Declaration of Human Rights?

    A. Lester Pearson

    B. Pierre Trudeau

    C. John Humphrey

    D. John Diefenbaker

17. Describe at least two of the responsibilities of the Ontario Human Rights Commission.

_____

_____

_____

_____

_____

_____

18. Former Supreme Court of Canada Justice Louise Arbour served as Chief Prosecutor for the tribunal charging those who committed war crimes in Bosnia in the 1990s. Which of the following of her positions was **most** controversial?

    A. France was negligent in arresting war criminals

    B. Canadian troops were also guilty of war crimes

    C. There is no such thing as a "war crime;" all war is a crime

    D. The United Nations was part of the problem, not the solution

19. Explain the conflict between Canada and the U.S. over the voyage of the *Manhattan* in 1969. Also explain the outcome of that conflict.

_____

_____

_____

_____

_____

_____

Use the following information to answer the next question.

Speaker I	I am happy we have found cures and treatments for deadly diseases that have been around for a long time, but I wonder if some of the things we do could cause new, deadlier diseases.
Speaker II	I am happy that my crops are pest-resistant. We work long and hard, and if the weather gives us a break, we make a living.
Speaker III	The doctors were able to detect the cancer a lot earlier than when my father was my age. I am lucky that I again have a long life expectancy.
Speaker IV	It appeared that we were going to be a childless couple. However, we were able to go to a fertility clinic, and now we have twins: a boy and a girl.

20. Which speaker has mixed feelings about biotechnology?

A. Speaker I

B. Speaker II

C. Speaker III

D. Speaker IV

ANSWERS AND SOLUTIONS FOR PRACTICE QUESTIONS

1. OR	6. OR	11. B	16. C
2. OR	7. B	12. OR	17. OR
3. A	8. OR	13. OR	18. A
4. OR	9. C	14. C	19. OR
5. D	10. OR	15. OR	20. A

1. Open Response

Prior to World War I, Canada wanted immigrants from Europe to help settle the West. During the Great Depression, unemployment was high, so immigration was extremely limited. In fact, emigration *out of* Canada was higher.

2. Open Response

The Canada-U.S. Free Trade Agreement (FTA) was created to give Canada and the U.S. open access to each other's markets for goods. It also dealt with concerns regarding energy, movement of people for business, and investments. The FTA led to NAFTA (North American Free Trade Agreement). Both of these agreements have pros and cons for each country, as well as supporters and detractors in each country.

The Canada-U.S. Free Trade Agreement (FTA) was negotiated and signed by Progressive Conservative Prime Minister Brian Mulroney's government. In the 1988 federal election, both the NDP and Liberals fought against the FTA, believing the U.S. economy would overwhelm the Canadian economy. Even though the Liberals were against the FTA, Prime Minister Jean Chrétien did not cancel the North American Free Trade Agreement (NAFTA) when they took power in 1993. It came into effect in 1994. Liberal Prime Minister Pierre Trudeau, for most of the period of 1968 to 1984, had no part in the FTA.

3. A

Clifford Sifton was Wilfrid Laurier's Minister of the Interior in the early 20th century. His free land policy helped settle Western Canada with Americans, Brits, Germans, Swedes, Ukrainians, and Dutch, among others.

4. Open Response

After World War II, Canada experienced a baby boom. Suburbs grew up in the 1950s when cities became more congested and polluted, while, at the same time, cars and other forms of public transportation became more available. Suburban life gave people an opportunity to live in larger homes with larger yards. To a certain extent, suburbs allowed people to live among those of a similar socio-economic status.

5. D

People are reluctant to support the construction of nuclear power stations because they associate them with nuclear weapons. The selection states the positive things about nuclear energy, including lower costs and fewer emissions. Another benefit is that four decades have passed without any member of the public being harmed by nuclear power in Canada.

6. **Open Response**

   The Balfour Report acknowledged that there were many global changes following World I. Britain was willing to give total sovereignty to those parts of the Empire (including Canada) that had achieved self-governing status.

7. **B**

   Canada is not a member of the European Union, but Canada has important economic, political, and social ties to the EU.

   Canada has been a member of the United Nations since its creation and is a member of the Commonwealth of Nations. Canada is also a member of La Francophonie, which is a group of countries united by the French language. The 12th Francophonie Summit will take place in Quebec City on October 17 to 19, 2008.

8. **Open Response**

   After World War II, people displaced by the war were seeking refuge in Canada. As well, after uprisings in Hungary in the 1950s, people looked to Canada for a new home in which to rebuild their lives.

9. **C**

   By the late 1950s to early 1960s, Canada's population was growing rapidly. The ability to fill occupational needs was the most important criteria of the Immigration Act of 1962.

10. **Open Response**

    Today, there are fears that Canada's pension fund and healthcare system will be severely depleted and burdened by the aging baby boomers.

11. **B**

    The least likely result of new technology is a lower standard of living.

    New technology tends to lower prices of products because they become less expensive to make. A rapid depletion of resources can occur when demand is high. Another result of new technology is a loss of certain types of jobs, but also a gain of other kinds of jobs.

12. **Open Response**

    Elsie MacGill was the first Canadian woman to earn a degree in electrical engineering and the first woman in North America to be awarded a master's degree in aeronautical engineering. Elsie became the chief aeronautical engineer at Canadian Car and Foundry and was head of production of the Hawker Hurricane fighter plane during World War II.

13. **Open Response**

    The Avro Arrow was an all-weather jet that was one of the fastest and most sophisticated fighter jets of its time. It was developed entirely in Canada at a cost of over $400 million in the 1950s. Over 13 000 people were employed in all aspects of its production. The cost to produce each plane was supposed to be $2 million; however, the cost jumped to $12.5 million per plane, which was deemed too expensive. Prime Minister Diefenbaker cancelled the project in 1959.

14. **C**

    The Statute of Westminster gave the dominions, including Canada, sovereignty.

    The British North America Act created the Dominion of Canada in 1867. The War Measures Act of 1914 empowered the federal government to take away some freedoms in an emergency. The Treaty of Versailles was the peace agreement ending World War I.

15. Open Response

On United Nations' missions, Canada has been both a peacekeeper and a peacemaker. Canadians are often called to work for specific UN agencies or programs. For example, Louise Arbour, a former Supreme Court of Canada Justice, served as a UN war crimes prosecutor from 1996 to 1999. Canadian doctors work with the WHO, which is the public health division of the United Nations.

16. C

Montreal lawyer John Humphrey represented Canada when the Universal Declaration of Human Rights was drawn up.

Prime Minister Lester Pearson is known for his role in foreign affairs. Prime Minister John Diefenbaker was involved in the establishment of the 1962 Bill of Rights. Prime Minister Pierre Trudeau was involved with the 1982 Charter of Rights and Freedoms.

17. Open Response

Human rights apply to all people equally. The goal of the Ontario Human Rights Commission is to ensure such a belief is a reality. Some of the responsibilities handled by the Commission are: investigating complaints filed by people in Ontario jails, investigating allegations of harassment in the workplace, and attempting to prevent discrimination by educating the public.

18. A

Louise Arbour believed that France made the situation in Bosnia worse by not arresting war criminals.

19. Open Response

Canadian sovereignty over the coastal waters of the Arctic Ocean was challenged in 1969 when the U.S. used the Northwest Passage and waters within Canadian jurisdiction to transport oil in the *Manhattan* from Alaska to New York.

The United States filed a complaint against Canada to the World Court, and an international conference convened. The issue was not resolved because the U.S. decided it was less expensive to transport oil from Alaska down the west coast. The issue of sovereignty remains unresolved.

20. A

Speaker I fears that people may be doing long-term damage; the long term effects of the combination of biology and technology are unknown.

UNIT TEST

1. Which of the following statements regarding immigration to Canada in the 1930s is **true**?
   A. Only refugees were accepted because of the Depression
   B. The number of immigrants was reduced slightly because of the Depression
   C. There was no new immigration, and 30 000 immigrants were sent back to Europe
   D. Immigration was encouraged because new immigrants would stimulate the economy

2. In which of the following countries did Canada demonstrate leadership by providing assistance during a crisis without also being implicated in some wrongdoing?
   A. Ethiopia
   B. Somalia
   C. Rwanda
   D. Bosnia

3. State the three main purposes of the Immigration Act of 1978.

   _____

   _____

   _____

   _____

   _____

   _____

4. The word *suburban* is used to describe communities that
   A. are neither rural nor urban
   B. have high-density populations
   C. are on the verge of becoming cities
   D. are located on the outskirts of cities

5. The baby boom occurred approximately between
   A. 1914 and 1945
   B. 1945 and 1965
   C. 1965 and 1985
   D. 1985 and 2005

6. Describe how housing and immigration were affected as the baby boomers grew up in the late 1960s.

_____

_____

_____

_____

_____

_____

7. Explain how new technology has affected working conditions in Canada.

_____

_____

_____

_____

_____

8. State Sir Frederick Banting's major contribution to medicine.

_____

_____

_____

_____

_____

_____

9. Explain why the Statute of Westminster, passed in 1931, was important for Canada.

_____

_____

_____

_____

_____

10. Which of the following statements about the Commonwealth of Nations is **false**?

   A. Both Canada and the United States are members

   B. There are over 50 member nations from every continent

   C. Both developed and less developed countries are member nations

   D. The population of the Commonwealth is approximately 1.7 billion

11. Describe the key details about the International Campaign to Ban Landmines. Include in your response the interesting point about the position of the U.S.

_____

_____

_____

_____

_____

12. Which of the following statements about both the genocide in the Ukraine and the Holocaust is **false**?
   A. Both events began in the 1930s.

   B. Both are considered to be man-made tragedies.

   C. Canada did little to help the victims while these events were occurring.

   D. Canada did as much as possible to take in Ukrainian and Jewish refugees.

13. The Human Rights Act of 1977 did **not** include freedom from discrimination based on
   A. race

   B. ethnic origin

   C. sexual preference

   D. physical disabilities

14. Explain how technology has changed the everyday lives of Canadians by comparing your life to that of a teenager from the early 1900s.

_____

_____

_____

_____

_____

15. Describe how technological advances changed warfare in the twentieth century and how those changes have affected civilians.

_____

_____

_____

_____

_____

_____

ANSWERS AND SOLUTIONS FOR UNIT TEST

1. C	5. B	9. OR	13. C
2. A	6. OR	10. A	14. OR
3. OR	7. OR	11. OR	15. OR
4. D	8. OR	12. D	

1. C

The economy in the 1930s was in such bad shape that there were not enough jobs; 30 000 immigrants were sent back to Europe between 1930 and 1935.

2. A

In 1984, when the world first became aware of the famine in Ethiopia, the Mulroney government sent foreign minister Joe Clark to Ethiopia. Canada became a world leader in sending food and money to assist Ethiopians.

Sadly, in Somalia, the Canadian military was disgraced by its scandalous involvement in the torture and death of a 16-year-old boy in 1993. In Rwanda, Canada, and the world, did not respond to Canadian Major-General Roméo Dallaire when he pleaded for more United Nations' help in dealing with the violence that ultimately led to the massacre of over 800 000 people. As well, there were allegations that a small group of Canadian soldiers abused their power in Bosnia.

3. Open Response

The Immigration Act of 1978 had three goals: promoting family reunion, upholding humanitarian values, and encouraging economic growth in Canada.

4. D

The word *suburban* refers to communities on the edges or outskirts of the city. Suburbs are part of the city but have lower population density, larger single family homes, and more parks.

5. B

The baby boom refers to the period between 1945 and 1965 when for 20 consecutive years the birth rate was over 20 births per 1 000 population. According to Statistics Canada, the birth rate has for the most part been in decline since then. By the late 1980s, it approached 16 births per 1 000 population.

6. Open Response

When the boomers started to marry and buy houses, housing prices rose due to supply and demand. More teachers were needed to educate the boomers; thus, immigration policies were changed in the early 1960s so that specialists, such as teachers, could immigrate to Canada.

7. Open Response

Technology has affected working conditions because certain jobs were eliminated as technology replaced people in some areas. Other jobs to do with newer technology have been created that pay well. Labour unions are still quite active in protecting workers.

8. **Open Response**

Sir Frederick Banting was one of the Canadians involved in the discovery of insulin, used to treat diabetes.

9. **Open Response**

Until the Statute of Westminster was passed in 1931, Canada was legally part of the British Empire; as such, the Canadian constitution was under the control of the British parliament, and could only be amended by that parliament. Since 1931, Canada has been totally sovereign and equal to Britain in the British Commonwealth.

10. **A**

The United States is not a member of the Commonwealth of Nations.

All the members of the Commonwealth were part of the British Empire until at least the end of the first quarter of the 20th century.

11. **Open Response**

The International Campaign to Ban Landmines is a coalition of non-governmental organizations established to end the destruction on civilians caused by landmines. In Ottawa in 1997, 125 countries signed a treaty agreeing to clear landmines in their territories within 10 years. As of 2008, 156 member states have signed the treaty, while 39 nations have not. The U.S. numbers among those who have *not*.

12. **D**

Canada did not do as much as possible to take in Ukrainian and Jewish refugees.

Like most of the world, Canada did little in 1932 to 1933 to assist those affected by the famine Josef Stalin created in the Ukraine. From 1933 until the beginning of World War II, the Canadian government did very little to take in Jewish refugees before the Holocaust, even though Adolf Hitler allowed some Jews to leave.

13. **C**

The Human Rights Act of 1977 did not list discrimination based on sexual preference.

The Act established an anti-discrimination code based on the grounds of race, national or ethnic origin, colour, religion, sex, age, marital status, physical disabilities, or past criminal convictions.

14. **Open Response**

In the early 1900s, much of the technology we take for granted had not been developed. Cars and airplanes were just starting to be invented. There were no radios or televisions, and certainly no computers or the Internet. The lives of teenagers from the early 1900s would have been, at the very least, quieter.

Today's teenagers are flooded by sounds, from MP3 players, to televisions, to the Internet, to video games. Technology was supposed to make our lives simpler, and it has, in some ways. We don't have to haul water into the house, or go outside to use the washroom. But, with instant communication, people's lives are busier and more hectic than ever, and, ironically, people often feel less connected to other *people*.

15. **Open Response**

War used to be a very hands-on battle. With advancements in technology, warfare is able to be conducted from thousands of miles away. Missiles and bombs can be used to kill with minimal risk to the soldiers deploying those weapons; however, these same technologies also result in more civilian casualties because of missed targets and targets based on inaccurate information. With the use of weapons such as landmines, the destructive impact of warfare on civilians can last much longer than the war itself.

Class Focus
Citizenship and Heritage

TABLE OF CORRELATIONS

Strand	General Expectation	Specific Outcome	Practice Questions	Unit Test
3 Citizenship and Heritage	3.1 describe the impact of significant social and political movements on Canadian society	3.1.1 summarize the key contribution of women's movements in Canada since 1914	1, 3	1, 6
		3.1.2 identify key struggles and contribution of the labour movement in Canada as well as key contributions of selected labour leaders	4	2, 8
		3.1.3 describe some of the factors shaping the experience of Aboriginal peoples in Canada since 1914 and ways in which Aboriginal people have worked to achieve recognition of Aboriginal and treaty rights	7, 8, 15	5
		3.1.4 compare the different beliefs and values of selected political parties that emerged out of political movements	2, 5, 6, 9	3, 4, 9, 10
	3.2 describe how individual Canadians have contributed to the development of Canada and its emerging sense of identity	3.2.1 describe how selected significant individuals have contributed to the growing sense of Canadian identity since 1914	10, 11, 13	
		3.2.2 describe how the work of selected artists has reflected Canadian identity	12, 14	7

CITIZENSHIP AND HERITAGE

SOCIAL AND POLITICAL MOVEMENTS

3.1.1   summarize the key contributions of women's movements in Canada since 1914

WOMEN'S MOVEMENTS IN CANADA SINCE 1914.

- **Suffrage/Franchise:** The right to vote.
- **Famous five** : A group consisting of Emily Murphy, Henrietta Muir Edwards, Louise McKinney, Irene Parlby, and Nellie McClung. They fought for the recognition of women as persons under the British North America Act. This group of women campaigned in several provinces and federally to help women gain the right to vote.
- **Widow:** A woman whose husband has died.
- **Spinster:** an unmarried woman (usually past the usual age to marry).

Women's groups made huge contributions in Canada during the 20th century. In the early 1900s, not only did women *not* have the right to vote, but women and their children were considered to be the property of their husbands. Women could not own land, and the money that they earned belonged to their husbands.

Early in the first decade of the 20th century, the women's suffrage movement began in Ontario and the four western provinces of Manitoba, Saskatchewan, Alberta, and British Columbia. At first, some women (usually widows and spinsters) were allowed to vote in municipal (local) elections. Women's suffrage groups were pushing for the right to vote in both provincial and federal elections. The first provinces to grant women the right to vote were Manitoba in January 1916, Saskatchewan in March 1916, and Alberta in April 1916. On May 24, 1918, all female citizens aged 21 and over became eligible to vote in federal elections, regardless of whether they had yet attained the provincial franchise.

In 1929, the Famous Five fought for the recognition of women as people under the British North America Act. The success of the Famous Five and other women's groups resulted in women being able to be appointed to the Canadian Senate and other government jobs. Women in all provinces fought for better conditions and rights for women specifically regarding property rights, wages, and working conditions.

In 1970, the Royal Commission on the Status of Women report recommended that the federal government take steps to ensure equal opportunities for women in society and the workplace. Section six of the Charter of Rights and Freedoms, which came into effect in 1982, wrote into the constitution that men and women were to be treated equally "before and under the law." An ongoing issue for women is receiving equal pay for the same work as men.

Despite this legal protection, women are still subjected to violence. The Canadian government proclaimed December 6 a National Day of Remembrance and Action on Violence Against Women, in memory of the fourteen women who were killed on that date in 1989 at the University of Montreal, and all women harmed by violence against women.

3.1.2 identify key struggles and contributions of the labour movement in Canada.

LABOUR MOVEMENT AND LABOUR LEADERS

- **The Labour movement**: Collective organizations of working people.
- **Strike:** When workers withdraw their services in order to negotiate better working conditions.
- **Capitalism:** Private ownership of the means of production.
- **Democratic socialism**: Public ownership of the means of production.
- **Social programs:** Government programs to assist those in need.

The labour movement has forced many social, economic, and political changes. The Winnipeg General Strike began on May 2, 1919 by workers in factories, and two weeks later, included approximately 30 000 to 35 000 workers in virtually all the trades and occupations. The strike only ended in mid-June when the federal government intervened and arrested the union leaders, including J.S. Woodsworth, who was to become a Winnipeg Labour Member of Parliament in 1921.

During the Great Depression of the 1930s, relief camp workers went on strike, and about 1 000 of them commandeered freight trains to Ottawa to meet with Prime Minister R.B. Bennett. This On-to-Ottawa Trek, as it was called, led to fears of a communist revolution, so the Prime Minister had the Royal Canadian Mounted Police stop the strikers at Regina, where a riot broke out.

Also during the Great Depression in 1933, a few MPs, as well as some university professors and leaders of farmers' organizations, met in Regina where they adopted the Regina Manifesto, creating the Cooperative Commonwealth Federation (CCF). This new political party attacked what it felt to be the negatives of capitalism and argued in favour of democratic socialism. In 1961, the CCF was to merge with the Canadian Labour Congress, which represented 80% of all union members, to form the New Democratic Party (NDP). Over the last half of the 20th century, the CCF/NDP has never governed Canada, but has been successful in getting governments to spend money on social programs.

Another powerful labour union in Canada is the Canadian Auto Workers, formed by Bob White in 1985.

These unions and groups have affected change in Canada by creating limits on time worked, health and safety legislations, minimum wages, and employment standards.

3.1.3 describe some of the factors shaping the experience of Aboriginal peoples in Canada since 1914 Aboriginal people have worked to achieve recognition of Aboriginal and treaty rights

SOCIAL AND DEMOGRAPHIC CHANGE ON ABORIGINAL COMMUNITIES

- **Aboriginal:** First known occupants of a country; i.e., Aboriginal People.
- **Residential schools:** Boarding schools for the purpose of trying to assimilate First Nations people.

Aboriginal People have struggled with their experiences within Canada, and Aboriginal communities of Canada have been victimized by discriminatory government policies. It was the policy of the federal government to try to assimilate Aboriginal People into white culture. This assimilation was attempted through residential schools and the banning of traditional ceremonies.

Relocation, urbanization, education, and assimilation attempts changed the way Aboriginal People had traditionally lived, wreaking havoc on their cultures. This loss of culture has had a huge impact on the lives of all Aboriginal People and continues to cause problems for their way of life today.

Two examples of harmful policies are relocation and residential schools. In the 1950s, an Inuit community in Northern Quebec was relocated to the High Arctic; they were unable to successfully re-establish their lifestyles, and they were not given help to return to their homes. As Canada urbanized in the 1920s, the rights of Aboriginal People were taken away. Probably the most devastating policy was the implementation of residential schools. The lasting impact of these schools for many Aboriginal People was drug abuse, domestic violence, and a loss of pride and self-respect.

For some Aboriginal communities, taking back control of their own schools, health clinics, and child welfare agencies and bringing back traditional forms of self-government has started to create a sense of autonomy and pride in their communities.

RECOGNITION OF THE RIGHTS OF ABORIGINAL PEOPLES IN CANADA

- **Status Indians**: Indians registered on an official federal list.
- **First Nations** : All Aboriginals that are not Inuit or Métis.

The Union of Ontario Indians was formed in 1919 to represent the 42 Anishinabek First Nations of Ontario in political matters with the Ontario government. Aboriginal rights groups in the 1970s and 1980s were formed to try to deal with issues related to poverty, discrimination, and the conditions of abusive residential schools of the past.

The Inuit Tapiriit Kanatami was formed in 1971 to represent Canada's 40 000 Inuit in matters related to language, cultural protection, and land claims. The Assembly of First Nations (AFN), which came together in 1982, is the national organization representing Status Indians and First Nations people. They were a powerful advocate against the Meech Lake accord and were included in conferences leading up to the 1992 Charlottetown Accord, which also failed to be accepted by Canadians.

The National Aboriginal Veterans Association (NAVA) tries to help Aboriginal People who have served in wars or the Armed Forces on behalf of Canada in different ways, such as scholarships for their children's education.

3.1.4   compare the different beliefs and values of selected political parties that emerged out of political movements

THE ROLE OF MOVEMENTS

• **Traditional political parties:** The Liberals. The Progressive Conservatives

During the Great Depression, three new political movements were born largely because many people felt the traditional political parties were not able to solve Canada's economic problems. These new political movements included the Cooperative Commonwealth Federation (CCF) in Saskatchewan, the Social Credit Party in Alberta, and the Union Nationale in Quebec.

All were to form governments in several different provinces (CCF/NDP in Saskatchewan, British Columbia, Manitoba, and Ontario; Social Credit in Alberta and British Columbia; and Union Nationale in Quebec). The CCF, which became the New Democratic Party in 1961, had a major impact federally on the development of social legislation.

In the late 1980s, the Reform Party of Canada arose in Western Canada because of the belief of many Western Canadians that the federal government was dominated by the traditional parties based in Ontario and Quebec.

Following the 1990 failure to approve the Meech Lake accord, several Liberal and Progressive Conservatives from Quebec formed the Bloc Québécois (BQ) to protect Quebec's interests at the federal level. In 1993, the BQ won enough seats to form the official Opposition.

In the 1997 election, the Reform Party achieved official Opposition status. In 2000, they became the Canadian Alliance, and in that year's election, they again won enough seats to form the official Opposition. In 2003, they merged with the Progressive Conservative Party to become the Conservative Party of Canada. In the 2006 election, they won enough seats to form a minority government.

The Green Party has been gaining political strength across Canada, and for the first time, the leader of the Green Party was allowed to participate in the federal election debate in 2008. Their platform of environmental responsibility combines some left-wing and some right-wing policies.

INDIVIDUAL CANADIANS AND CANADIAN IDENTITY

3.2.1   describe how selected significant individuals have contributed to the growing sense of Canadian identity since 1914

THE DEVELOPMENT OF THE CANADIAN IDENTITY SINCE 1914

When Canadians gain international recognition, Canada's sense of identity blossoms and grows. Several Canadians have earned international reputations for their accomplishments: Nellie McClung and Thérèse Casgrain fought for women's rights in the early part of the 20th century; Arthur Currie was the Canadian general who led the successful attack on Vimy Ridge during the First World War; Georges Vanier was Canada's first French-Canadian Governor General; and upon his death, his wife Pauline Vanier completed the term.

Additionally, Second World War pilot Max Ward created Wardair in the 1950s; In the 1960s, Marshall McLuhan coined the term *global village* because of the changes to the world brought about by television; Jamaican-born Rosemary Brown fought for women's rights and against racism; Matthew Coon Come was the National Chief of the Assembly of First Nations from 2000 to 2003 and led the fight for Aboriginal rights against the Quebec government regarding the James Bay hydroelectric project; Maurice Richard was the first National Hockey League player to score 50 goals in a 50-game season; and Adrienne Clarkson, an accomplished journalist, became Canada's first Governor General of Chinese descent.

3.2.2   describe how the work of selected artists has reflected Canadian Identity.

ARTISTIC EXPRESSION AND CANADIAN IDENTITY

- **The Group of Seven:** A group of Canadian landscape painters in the 1920s. The artists included Franklin Carmichael, Lawren Harris, A.Y. Jackson, Frank Johnston, Arthur Lismer, J.E.H. MacDonald, and Frederick Varley. Tom Thomson (who died in 1917) and Emily Carr were closely associated with and influenced by the group, though they were never officially members.

A nation's identity is often reflected by the work of its artists. A variety of Canadians have contributed to Canada's unique identity. Ozias Leduc, one of Quebec's early painters, and the Group of Seven were famous for painting Canadian landscapes in the 1920s.

Many writers have depicted different aspects of Canadian life. Farley Mowat described the difficulties of living in Northern Canada, while Gabrielle Roy described French-Canadian life. Joy Kogawa wrote about the Japanese internment during the Second World War. These are just three examples of the many Canadian authors who have won both national and international recognition.

Jazz pianist Oscar Peterson and rock and rollers the Guess Who both have international reputations as being among the all-time greatest in their fields. Chief Dan George, a musician and actor, achieved international acclaim for his role in the movie *Little Big Man*. Musician Susan Aglukark became the first person to receive the Aboriginal Achievement Award in the Arts and Entertainment field in 1994.

Some other Canadians who have received international recognition include ballerina Karen Kain, Olympic figure skater Toller Cranston, Sri Lankan-born writer Michael Ondaatje, and playwright/journalist Drew Hayden Taylor.

NOTES

PRACTICE QUESTIONS

Use the following information to answer the next question.

(Canadian Heritage) **Section 15** *Equality Rights*

1. **Every individual is equal before and under the law and has the right to the equal protection and equal benefit of the law without discrimination and, in particular, without discrimination based on race, national or ethnic origin, colour, religion, sex, age, or mental or physical disability.**

2. **Subsection (1) does not preclude any law, program, or activity that has as its object the amelioration of conditions of disadvantaged individuals or groups including those that are disadvantaged because of race, national or ethnic origin, colour, religion, sex, age, or mental or physical disability.**

This section of the Charter makes it clear that every individual in Canada—regardless of race, religion, national or ethnic origin, colour, sex, age, or physical or mental disability—is to be considered equal. This means that governments must not discriminate on any of these grounds in its laws or programs.

The Supreme Court of Canada has stated that the purpose of section 15 is to protect those groups who suffer social, political, and legal disadvantage in society. Discrimination occurs where, for example, a person suffers disadvantages or is denied opportunities available to other members of society because of a personal characteristic.

At the same time as it protects equality, the Charter also allows for certain laws or programs that favour disadvantaged individuals or groups. For example, programs aimed at improving employment opportunities for women, Aboriginal People, visible minorities, or those with mental or physical disabilities are allowed under section 15(2).

1. Explain why the Famous Five and other Suffragettes from the early 20th century would be excited by the *Equality Rights* section of the Charter.

   _____

   _____

   _____

   _____

   _____

   _____

2. Which of the following political movements began as a result of western Canadian discontent in the latter part of the 20th century?

   A. Social Credit

   B. New Democratic Party

   C. Reform Party of Canada

   D. Cooperative Commonwealth Federation

3. The **greatest** achievement of the Famous Five was that they
   A. led the fight for prohibition
   B. fought for women's voting rights
   C. represented women at the Charlottetown Conference
   D. fought for and won the right for women to be declared persons

4. Explain what led to the Winnipeg General Strike of 1919.

   _____
   _____
   _____
   _____
   _____

5. Which of the following people supported the concept of a democratic socialist society for Canada?
   A. R.B. Bennett
   B. William Aberhart
   C. James S. Woodsworth
   D. William Lyon Mackenzie King

6. Explain the Cooperative Commonwealth Federation—specifically, what the party is known as today, how it was created, and what its main beliefs are as a political party.

   _____
   _____
   _____
   _____
   _____

7. Explain three objectives of the Assembly of First Nations.

   _____
   _____
   _____
   _____
   _____

Use the following source to answer the next question.

Government of Canada Supports Inuit Tapiriit Kanatami

OTTAWA, February 18, 2005—Deputy Leader of the Government in the House of Commons and Member of Parliament (Ottawa-Vanier) Mauril Bélanger, on behalf of Minister of Canadian Heritage and Minister responsible for Status of Women Liza Frulla, today announced $389,667 in funding for the Inuit Tapiriit Kanatami (ITK). The funds will help the ITK to promote participation by Inuit in Canada's political, social and economic institutions.

"One of the Government of Canada's priorities is to ensure that Aboriginal people can influence decisions that affect their daily lives," said Mr. Bélanger. "Through the work of organizations such as the Inuit Tapiriit Kanatami, Inuit can make their voices heard and can build communities in which their way of life and languages are valued."

"I am pleased that we have renewed our partnership with the Inuit Tapiriit Kanatami," said Minister Frulla. "By encouraging Inuit to participate in all aspects of Canadian society, we draw on what they have to offer and facilitate the preservation of their heritage and the promotion of their culture, for the benefit of all Canadians."

The funding will enable the ITK to continue functioning as the representative organization for approximately 41,000 Inuit living in the Inuvialuit region, Nunavut, Nunavik, Labrador and elsewhere in Canada. The mandate of the ITK is to highlight the needs and aspirations of Inuit, and to preserve their identity, culture, languages and way of life.

Financial assistance is provided by the Department of Canadian Heritage through the Aboriginal Representative Organizations Program (AROP). AROP's objective is to maintain a consultative framework of Inuit, Métis and Non-Status Indian representative organizations through which governments can address social, economic, political and cultural issues affecting the lives of Aboriginal peoples in Canada. The program is managed by the Aboriginal Affairs Branch of the Department of Canadian Heritage.

Funding announced today was provided for in the March 2004 federal budget.

8. The Canadian Government hopes to

    A. assimilate the Inuit

    B. help the Inuit preserve and promote their culture

    C. build new housing for the Inuit in Northern Canada

    D. have the Inuit Tapiriit Kanatami join forces with the Assembly of First Nations

9. Describe the **most** important goal of the Bloc Québécois.

    _____

    _____

    _____

    _____

    _____

    _____

10. Which of the following people became Canada's first Governor General from a visible minority group?
    A. Georges Vanier
    B. Rosemary Brown
    C. Thérèse Casgrain
    D. Adrienne Clarkson

11. Which of the following statements **best** describes Aboriginal Matthew Coon Come?
    A. He was a founding member of the Assembly of First Nations
    B. He served with distinction in the Canadian army during the First World War
    C. He served with distinction in the Canadian Air Force during the Second World War
    D. He fought hard to ensure Aboriginal rights were preserved during both Meech Lake and Charlottetown constitutional discussions

12. Which of the following Canadian artists is known for writing?
    A. Karen Kain
    B. Farley Mowat
    C. Oscar Peterson
    D. Toller Cranston

13. Which of the following people has first-hand knowledge of Japanese internment during the Second World War?
    A. Joy Kogawa
    B. Gabrielle Roy
    C. Susan Aglukark
    D. Michael Ondaatje

14. Explain why the work of the Group of Seven was, and still is, important to Canadian identity.

    _____
    _____
    _____
    _____
    _____

15. Explain the purpose of the residential schools that Aboriginal People were forced to attend and describe some of the effects of those schools on First Nations' culture.

    _____
    _____
    _____
    _____
    _____

ANSWERS AND SOLUTIONS FOR PRACTICE QUESTIONS

1. OR	5. C	9. OR	13. A
2. C	6. OR	10. D	14. OR
3. D	7. OR	11. D	15. OR
4. OR	8. B	12. B	

1. Open Response

The Famous Five and other Suffragettes would be thrilled with the Equality Section in the Charter of Rights and Freedoms because it makes an effort to ensure that groups that have historically been discriminated against, including women, are treated equally.

2. C

The Reform Party was founded by Preston Manning in 1987. For the most part, they believed western issues were being ignored by the federal government.

Both the Social Credit in Alberta and the Cooperative Commonwealth Federation (CCF) began in the 1930s in the west largely due to the Great Depression. In 1961, the CCF became the New Democratic Party (after merging with the Canadian Labour Congress).

3. D

The Famous Five fought and won the right for women to be declared persons in 1929 when the British Privy Council overturned a decision made by the Supreme Court of Canada denying them this right.

4. Open Response

Following the First World War, the Canadian economy was slow to adjust to peacetime production. Prices rose rapidly during the war in 1918, and the inflation rate was 38%. Unemployment, especially among those who had returned from the war, was also a problem. There were allegations that many wealthy people became wealthier during the war by selling their products at inflated prices. Unions formed and pushed for wage increases to deal with inflation. Several different groups of workers in Winnipeg went on strike to try to influence the employers.

5. C

James S. Woodsworth had been an independent Member of Parliament since 1921 and was involved in the creation of the Regina Manifesto in 1933. This document created the Cooperative Commonwealth Federation (CCF), a political party that did believe in democratic socialism.

R.B. Bennett and William Mackenzie King were both Canadian prime ministers, and William Aberhart was premier of Alberta between 1935 and 1943.

6. **Open Response**

The Cooperative Commonwealth Federation (CCF) was created in 1933. This new political party attacked what it felt to be the negatives of capitalism and argued in favour of democratic socialism. In 1961, the CCF merged with the Canadian Labour Congress, which represented 80% of all union members, to form the New Democratic Party (NDP). Over the last half of the 20th century, the CCF/NDP has never governed Canada, but has been successful in getting governments to spend money on social programs.

7. **Open Response**

The Assembly of First Nations has several goals. Some examples of these objectives are as follows: 1) working toward resolving disputes regarding land claims; 2) putting an end to discrimination against Canada's aboriginals; 3) bringing about better health and living conditions for aboriginals; and 4) the protection of Aboriginal People and their culture.

8. **B**

Canada's government recognizes that the Inuit and other Aboriginal People have much to contribute to Canada, and in this instance, funding is being made available to help the Inuit preserve and promote their culture.

9. **Open Response**

The Bloc Québécois came into being as a federal political party in 1990 following the failure of the Canadian provinces to approve the Meech Lake accord. Its goal is to defend the interests of Quebec federally until such time as Quebec is able to gain its own sovereignty.

10. **D**

Adrienne Clarkson served as Governor General from 1999 to 2005. She was born in Hong Kong and came to Canada in 1942 at the age of 5.

Rosemary Brown was born in Jamaica and won election to the British Columbia legislature in 1972. Montreal-born Georges Vanier served as Governor General from 1959 to 1967. Thérèse Casgrain was known mostly for championing women's rights in Quebec, and later she campaigned against nuclear weapons.

11. **D**

Matthew Coon Come made significant contributions on behalf of Aboriginal rights at both the Meech Lake and Charlottetown accord discussions.

12. **B**

Farley Mowat wrote about his personal struggles with Canada's northern environment.

Karen Kain earned her fame as a ballet dancer, and Oscar Peterson achieved fame as a Jazz pianist. Toller Cranston won fame as a figure skater but is also an internationally renowned painter and illustrator.

13. **A**

Born in Vancouver in 1935, Joy Kogawa was sent to an internment camp in 1942.

Susan Aglukark is a noted Inuit singer. Michael Ondaatje is a writer who won the 1992 Governor General's Award for fiction, and Gabrielle Roy wrote about French-Canadian life.

14. Open Response

The work of the Group of Seven was and still is important to Canadian identity because they showed the world that Canadian landscapes were indeed worth painting. They became recognized as pioneers of a new school of art. When they disbanded, they created the Canadian Group of Painters, forever changing the landscape of Canadian art.

15. Open Response

The purpose of the residential schools that aboriginals were forced to attend was to ban all cultural traditions and language in hopes of assimilating the Native People into white culture.

The effect of those schools on First Nations culture is that many traditions and languages have been lost. Many First Nations people today feel disconnected from their elders and their culture because of the separation from family and banishment of traditions.

UNIT TEST

1. Explain the end result of the Persons' Case of 1929.

_____

_____

_____

_____

_____

Use the following information to answer the next question.

A student gathered the following facts:

- One Big Union
- Over 30 000 on strike
- Lasted from May to June 1919
- Federal Immigration Act amended

2. Which of the following titles is **most appropriate** for the student's report?

   A. "The Winnipeg General Strike"

   B. "The History of Canadian Unions"

   C. "The Labour Movement During the Depression"

   D. "The History of the Communist Party in Canada"

3. Give a brief biography of Tommy Douglas, including which political party he founded, which province he was premier of and during which years, and his most notable effect on Canada.

   _____

   _____

   _____

   _____

   _____

   _____

Use the following news report to answer the next question.

After the meeting, a party spokesman said that the new party had a goal of replacing the capitalist system because they believe that it has created inequalities of wealth and opportunity, and that too many people live in poverty. The goal, she said, was to create an economic system in which production and distribution are owned, controlled, and operated by the government. When asked about human rights, she stated that the party would not interfere with cultural, racial, or religious minorities; the party is a democratic movement made up of farmers and labourers and does not believe in violence like communism (July 1933).

4. To which Canadian political party could the news report apply?

A. Social Credit

B. Reform Party

C. Union Nationale

D. Cooperative Commonwealth Federation

5. Explain what event occurred in 1973 that led the Assembly of First Nations to become active in Canada's political affairs.

_____

_____

_____

_____

_____

_____

6. Describe one major accomplishment of TWO of the following women:

A. Irene Parlby

B. Emily Murphy

C. Nellie McClung

D. Henrietta Edwards

_____

_____

_____

_____

_____

_____

_____

_____

_____

_____

7. Which of the following statements is **not** true regarding the Group of Seven?

   A. The group was founded in 1920.

   B. The group met in Western Canada.

   C. There were actually more than 7 members in the group.

   D. The group members focused on painting Canadian landscapes.

8. Describe the unsuccessful On-to-Ottawa Trek of 1935.

   _____

   _____

   _____

   _____

   _____

   _____

9. Which of the following statements is **not** true about the Reform Party of Canada?

   A. It became the Canadian Alliance.

   B. It eventually merged with the Liberals.

   C. It was founded by Preston Manning in the late 1980s.

   D. It was based in Western Canada and addressed Western alienation.

10. Which prime minister spent the most time in office?

    A. Jean Chretien

    B. Brian Mulroney

    C. Pierre Elliot Trudeau

    D. William Lyon Mackenzie King

ANSWERS AND SOLUTIONS FOR UNIT TEST

1. OR	4. D	7. B	10. D
2. A	5. OR	8. OR	
3. OR	6. OR	9. B	

1. Open Response

In 1929, the result of the Person's Case was that women could be appointed to the Canadian Senate.

2. A

The best title for the report is "The Winnipeg General Strike." Because of inflation and the moderate policies of the Trade and Labour Congress, more radical elements formed One Big Union, and by mid-May, over 30 000 people were on strike, impacting hotels, restaurants, newspapers, and even the food supply. The federal Immigration Act was amended to allow the government to deport citizens not born in Canada. The strike became violent in mid-June, and amendments to the Criminal Code empowered the government to arrest and deport those suspected of being threats to security; union leaders were imprisoned, and the strike was brought to an end.

3. Open Response

Tommy Douglas was a founding member of the Cooperative Commonwealth Federation in 1933 and premier of Saskatchewan from 1944 to 1961. He is most famous for his strong support of Medicare, and while leading the federal New Democratic Party in the 1960s, he was able to influence Liberal minority Prime Minister Lester Pearson to introduce federal health care.

4. D

The fictional account is based on some of the statements contained in the Regina Manifesto of 1933, which created the Cooperative Commonwealth Federation.

5. Open Response

In 1973, Canada's top court recognized Aboriginal land claims, and since then, both provincial and federal governments have been compensating First Nations' groups. One of the goals of the Assembly of First Nations is to deal with land claims.

6. Open Response

All of the women listed were members of the Famous Five.

Irene Parlby was the first woman provincial cabinet minister.

Emily Murphy was, among other things, the first woman magistrate in Canada and the British Empire.

Nellie McClung helped give Manitoba women the vote and she served in Alberta's Legislative Assembly.

Henrietta Edwards helped found the National Council of Women in 1893.

7. B

The Group of Seven met each other in Toronto between 1911 and 1913.

The group was founded in 1920. After their first exhibition at the Art Gallery of Toronto in 1920, they began to identify themselves as a landscape school. The group was fluid; people left the group and others joined, and others were associated with the group.

8. Open Response

The On-to-Ottawa Trek of 1935 was when approximately 1 000 of the 1 500 striking workers left British Columbia by train and were joined by others. They were forced off the train by the Royal Canadian Mounted Police following Prime Minister Bennett's orders. Two thousand people arrived in Regina, and a public protest resulted in two deaths. The Trek ended with a riot in Regina in July 1835.

9. B

The Reform Party of Canada did not eventually merge with the Liberals.

The Reform Party of Canada was founded in the late 1980s by Preston Manning because of concerns related to Western alienation from the rest of Canada. It won opposition status in the 1997 federal election, and in 2000, they became the Canadian Alliance after a failed attempt to merge with the Progressive Conservatives. In 2003, the Alliance and the Progressive Conservatives successfully merged, forming the Conservative Party of Canada led by Stephen Harper. Harper and the Conservatives won a minority government in January 2006.

10. D

William Lyon Mackenzie King was Canada's longest serving prime minister. He was in office from 1921 to June 1926, September 1926 to 1930, and 1935 to 1948.

Pierre Elliot Trudeau served as prime minister from 1968 to 1979 and again from 1980 to 1984. Brian Mulroney served from 1984 to 1993. Jean Chretien served from 1993 to 2003.

Class Focus
Social, Economic, & Political Structures

TABLE OF CORRELATIONS

	Strand	General Expectation	Specific Outcome	Practice Questions	Unit Test
4	Social, Economic, and Political Structures	4.1 explain changing economic conditions and patterns and how they have affected Canadians	4.1.1 compare economic conditions at selected times in Canada's history and describe their impact on the daily lives of Canadians	1, 3, 4, 10	2, 4
			4.1.2 assess the advantages and disadvantages of American participation in the Canadian economy	5, 6	3
			4.1.3 identify some of the major effects of, and concerns arising with, free trade and globalization focusing on at least two groups	2, 7	
			4.1.4 identify the contributions of selected Canadian entrepreneurs and Canadian owned firms to the development of the Canadian economy	8, 9	5
		4.2 assess the changing role and power of the federal and provincial governments in Canada since 1914	4.2.1 explain why selected social welfare programs were established in Canada	13, 14, 15	1, 6, 8,.10
			4.2.2 assess key instances in which the Canadian government chose to restrict citizens' rights and freedoms, in wartime and peacetime	11, 12	7, 9
			4.2.3 identify how the federal government has used the media		

SOCIAL, ECONOMIC, AND POLITICAL STRUCTURES

THE INFLUENCE OF ECONOMIC STRUCTURES ON DAILY LIFE

4.1.1   compare economic conditions at selected times in Canada's history and describe their impact on the daily lives of Canadians.

ECONOMIC CONDITIONS IN CANADA'S HISTORY

- **Standard of living:** the ability to purchase many goods and services.
- **Depression:** a time when there is a large number of unemployed people and a reduction in spending and productivity.
- **Black Monday:** Monday, October 27, 1987, when markets around the world crashed. Markets in Canada and the United States dropped 22%.

The economy of Canada has seen many highs and lows. Some of the high times include the booming economy of the 1920s, the 1950s to the 1960s, and the 1980s. Some of the low times include the Great Depression in the 1930s, the turbulent 1970s with inflation and the oil crisis, the recession of the 1990s, and the dot-com bubble of 2000. Overall, the Canadian economy has had a huge impact on the daily lives of Canadians.

Economic Conditions of the 1920s and 1930s

There were several changes in the Canadian economy between the 1920s and what is referred to as the "dirty thirties." In the early 1920s, the Canadian economy, with the exception of the Maritime provinces, was prosperous and booming. Most people were employed and had money to spend on the many goods being produced. People were enjoying a higher standard of living when the economy went into a depression at the start of the 1930s.

Individuals struggled terribly during the Great Depression. The traditional political parties were not able to provide adequate relief for Canadians, and it was in this decade that three new political movements arose: the Cooperative Commonwealth Federation in Saskatchewan, the Social Credit Party in Alberta, and the Union Nationale in Quebec.

The 1950s and 1960s

The Canadian economy became prosperous after the First World War. The industries that had been developed to produce goods for the military were able to adapt quickly to the production of consumer goods. Advances in synthetic fibres, plastics, and electronics during the Second World War led to economic diversity and the growth of different types of industries. The prosperity of the 1950s was also fuelled by investment from the United States.

After the Second World War, the baby boom occurred and changed the economic landscape in Canada forever. The increase in babies and children changed the way companies created and marketed products. The population rise also meant that more doctors and teachers were needed to meet the demands of this growing population. Housing and transportation needs changed and increased. All of these factors created a booming economy through the 1950s and 1960s.

The 1970s

This decade saw a decline in the value of the Canadian dollar, high inflation, and high unemployment. The price of oil increased, meaning increased prices for oil, gas, and most consumer products (as a result of increased production costs). By the end of the decade, the interest rate was almost 20%.

The 1980s, 1990s, and 2000s

The beginning of the 1980s saw a continued struggle with the recession of the late 1970s, with high inflation and unemployment. The economy began to recover in the mid-1980s, but Black Friday in 1987 marked the beginning of a recession in Canada that lasted into the mid-1990s. The low interest rates of the late 1990s allowed venture capitalists to extravagantly start "dot-com" companies (in the Internet and computer industry), often ignoring good business practices. In early 2000, stock prices for these new companies soared, despite the lack of proven track records. The sheer number of startup companies meant that there would be large numbers of failures as well. By the end of 2002, more than half of these companies no longer existed.

4.1.2   assess the advantages and disadvantages of American participation in the Canadian economy

AMERICAN PARTICIPATION IN THE CANADIAN ECONOMY

- **Branch plants:** a company in Canada that is owned and controlled by Americans
- **Media:** radio, television, and newspapers
- **Depleted:** used up

The United States conducts a lot of business in Canada, and there are both positive and negative consequences associated with this. For example, many American companies set up branch plants. This could mean that actions taken by the head office of the company in the United States might not necessarily be in Canada's best economic interests. On the other hand, foreign investment creates jobs for Canadians.

Much of the entertainment and media in Canada comes from the United States. The Canadian government has had to enact laws protecting Canada's cultural industries; however, the American entertainment industry often uses Canadian sites and crews to produce television and movies, which creates jobs and helps the economy.

There are several trade agreements and pacts between Canada and the United States that are reviewed and updated periodically in an attempt to maintain an equitable trade arrangement for both countries; however, these agreements are often difficult to negotiate and maintain because of the different interests and values of each country. To ensure fish stocks are not depleted too rapidly, Canada has declared a limit from its borders to the Atlantic and Pacific Oceans of approximately 320 kilometres. There has also been a dispute related to trade in softwood lumber between Canada and the United States.

4.1.3   identify some of the major effects of, and concerns arising with, free trade and globalization

FREE TRADE AND GLOBALIZATION

Economic globalization is widespread, as countries try to compete in the ever-expanding global market. After the Second World War, the attitude of the world changed toward thinking globally. This change in attitude combined with technology gave birth to multinational and transnational companies that are the giants of today, such as General Motors, IBM, and Nike. These companies identified specific regions in the world where they could access resources and develop specific products at substantially diminished costs. The result was growing interdependence and new jobs in the developing world. It also meant a loss of employment in developed nations that were no longer competitive.

The World Trade Organization works to increase global trade and improve the economies of the world that are struggling to compete. The WTO, previously known as GATT (General Agreement on Tariffs and Trade), works to establish rules and regulations for international economic issues and acts as a mediator when disputes arise.

The G7/G8 is a group of countries with the wealthiest economies in the world who discuss issues of international economic importance as well as the impact international economic decisions may have on social and environmental conditions around the world. Both organizations face criticism from human rights and environmental activists, who feel that the groups work only to benefit their members, who are primarily wealthy and developed countries, while ignoring the issues faced by developing countries. Also, critics feel that issues about pollution are ignored, as well as human rights issues, such as child labour and poor wages.

Another example of economic globalization was the signing of the North American Free Trade Agreement (NAFTA), which came into effect in 1994. This agreement between Canada, the United States, and Mexico aimed to reduce all trade barriers between the three countries by 2008, although it is unlikely this will occur; however, exports and investments between the countries have increased significantly since the implementation of the agreement. Critics of the agreement feel it has hurt the Canadian economy, as several companies have moved their manufacturing plants to Mexico where labour and environmental standards are much less stringent. Critics also claim that the citizens of Mexico are being exploited by being subjected to poor working conditions and low wages.

Globalization of the economy has also meant that governments must ensure the safety of a huge amount of food and products that come from other countries. There have been several cases of disease and tainted products entering the Canadian marketplace from other parts of the world, as well as from within Canada. People expect that the products they purchase maintain a high level of safety, and it falls to the government to create standards and inspection agencies to keep Canadians safe. The mad cow disease crisis has had a huge impact on the Canadian economy, again showing the interdependence of today's global economic ties.

*4.1.4   identify the contributions of selected Canadian entrepreneurs and Canadian owned firms to the
         development of the Canadian economy*

CANADIAN ENTREPRENEURS AND CANADIAN-OWNED CORPORATIONS

• Entrepreneurs: business people that risk their own money on a business.

Although governments undertake some huge economic tasks, entrepreneurs are the cornerstones in
Canada's mixed economic system. One successful industrialist in the liquor industry is Samuel Bronfman.
His company, Seagram, was until recently the largest distiller of alcohol in the world. K.C. Irving was in
the oil and gas industry and was a major provider of oil and gas in Atlantic Canada and Quebec. George Weston
began life as a baker in the 19th century; today, his heirs control Loblaws, Canada's largest food distributor.
Ted Rogers Jr. has turned Rogers Communication into one of the largest companies in Canada. He also
owns the Toronto Blue Jays baseball team. Heather Reisman founded Indigo Books in 1996; in 2001,
Indigo Books merged with Chapters to become Canada's largest bookstore chain. Frank Stronach immigrated
to Canada in 1954 and is now a billionaire, employing over 80 000 people in his companies. In Quebec,
Pierre Péladeau founded Quebecor, which is the second largest printing company in the world. The Power
Corporation of Canada was created in 1925, and it's creators have significant investments in the electrical
power industry as well as in pulp and paper, media, and financial services. The Canadian Pacific Railway,
built in the last quarter of the 19th century, links Canada from coast to coast.

CHANGING ROLE AND POWER OF GOVERNMENTS

4.2.1   explain why selected social welfare programs were established in Canada.

SOCIAL WELFARE PROGRAMS

• **Social programs:** government programs to assist those in need.
• **Old age pensions:** an allowance for people who are retired.
• **Family allowance payments:** a set amount of money per child given to the child's mother.
• **Social welfare safety net:** all the programs provided by the government.
• **Deficits**: spending more than is collected.

Social welfare programs in Canada are controversial and expensive, but they are considered by many to
be a cornerstone of Canadian identity. Governments from all views of the political spectrum have tried
to balance the need and desire for costly social welfare programs with the higher taxes needed to fund
those programs. It is a difficult task and one in which not everyone will be happy with the results.

Old age pensions were introduced as early as 1927, but it was not until 1965 that the Canada Pension
Plan was created. It was created mainly because Liberal Prime Minister Lester B. Pearson had a minority
government and needed the support of the New Democratic Party, led by Tommy Douglas, to retain power.
In 1940, the Canadian government created the Unemployment Insurance Commission, now called the
Canada Employment Insurance Commission, to assist people out of work. Family allowance payments
began in 1945 to help with the costs of raising children. In 1968, the Pearson government introduced
Medicare, in which the costs of medical services would be shared by the federal and provincial governments,
not the individual receiving medical treatment.

Providing this social welfare safety net is expensive and has been a cause of government deficits. In the
late 1980s, Canada's Progressive Conservative government, led by Prime Minister Brian Mulroney,
began to reduce expenditures on social programs rather than increase taxes, and when Jean Chrétien
and the Liberals gained office in 1993, they continued this trend.

We don't have all the answers.

Just more answers than any other university in Canada.

With more world-leading researchers, in more fields, teaching 841 distinct undergraduate, 520 graduate and 42 professional programs, U of T is Canada's leader in answering the world's toughest questions. And we're educating this country's brightest to do the same.

UNIVERSITY OF
TORONTO
www.utoronto.ca

teacher.
entrepreneur.
problem solver.
designer.
leader.

The Schulich Engineer.

At the Schulich School of Engineering, we inspire students to be more than highly skilled engineers.

Visit www.schulich.ucalgary.ca to find out more.

SCHULICH
School of Engineering

UNIVERSITY OF
CALGARY

U OF C
THIS IS NOW

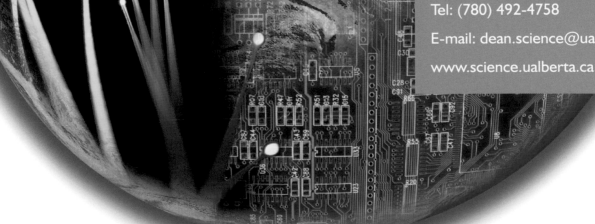

Helping to keep more people healthier longer

York's Faculty of Health will help you gain a deeper understanding of people. Our health and human science programs range from the molecular to the global. We'll provide you with insights into the broader factors determining the health of individuals, countries and whole populations.

School of Health Policy & Management
The only school of its kind. Explore health from an interdisciplinary perspective. The Honours Bachelor of Health Studies (BHS degree) is offered in Health Management, Health Informatics and Health Policy.

School of Kinesiology & Health Science
Study human movement and the relationship between physical activity and health. We offer both the Bachelor of Arts (BA) and Bachelor of Science (BSc) degrees.

School of Nursing
Patient centered learning in a dynamic and collaborative setting. Earn a Bachelor of Science (BScN) in Nursing.

Psychology
Canada's largest selection of psychology courses offered by world renowned educators and researchers. Both three and four-year degrees are offered including the Bachelor of Arts (BA) and Bachelor of Science (BSc).

Visit www.yorku.ca/health or Call at 416 736-5124

YORK UNIVERSITÉ UNIVERSITY U50
redefine THE POSSIBLE.

4.2.2 assess key instances in which the Canadian government chose to restrict citizens' rights and freedoms, in wartime and peacetime

RESTRICTIONS DURING WARTIME

- **War Measures Act:** a law giving the government sweeping powers during a national emergency that sometimes conflict with human rights.
- **Enemy aliens:** immigrants whose loyalty to Canada is questioned.
- **Internment camps:** a place where people were imprisoned without trial, usually for political reasons.
- **Conscription:** compulsory military service.
- **Centralized planning:** government management of the economy.
- **Crown corporations:** government-controlled companies, not private industry.
- **Censorship:** limits to free speech.
- **Rationing:** limiting the amount of consumer goods people can buy.

During both World Wars, the Canadian government limited some of the traditional rights and freedoms of their own citizens. In 1915, during the First World War, the government enacted the War Measures Act and reacted to public fears by placing more than 8 000 enemy aliens into internment camps. Internment occurred again during the Second World War; about 22 000 Japanese Canadians were interned. Also during the First World War, the Military Services Act introduced conscription, and during the Second World War, the National Resources Mobilization Act (1940) gave the government the power to introduce conscription again.

During the Second World War, the government became very active and introduced a high degree of centralized planning. For example, the National Selective Service was created by the government to tell Canadians where they would be employed; failure to comply could mean a $500 fine and a year in jail. Crown corporations produced munitions, airplanes, uniforms, and other necessities of war. Strikes and lockouts were illegal during the war, and there was censorship. Rationing was introduced in order to use most of the available resources for the production of items necessary for the war.

Following the wars, rights and freedoms were returned. In 1988, the Canadian parliament officially apologized to Japanese Canadians and gave each survivor $21 000.

4.2.3   identify how the federal government has used the media.

METHODS TO PROMOTE NATIONAL IDENTITY

In order to create a sense of Canadian identity, the federal government has created symbols and organizations that promote a national identity. Symbolism is used to help people in Canada feel a sense of belonging and sameness with other Canadians. For example, the Maple Leaf is a symbol that is internationally recognized as Canadian, and many Canadians feel it is a way of defining who they are. Both at home and abroad, many Canadians feel a sense of pride and nationhood when they see a Maple Leaf or wear one
on their clothing. It helps to identify them as Canadian, and it is something that only Canadians share. The Canadian national anthem is an auditory symbol that again creates national pride when heard.

Institutions can also promote a national identity. Some institutions influence the way the international community views a country, or they are closely associated with the history of a country. An institution that works to promote Canadian identity is the Canadian Broadcasting Corporation (CBC). The CBC is
a media institution that provides information to Canadians about important issues through the Internet, radio, and television. Information from the CBC is available in both French and English, and the CBC works to promote the achievements of Canadians in a broad spectrum of activities. For Canadians, it is
a source of news about the government as well as about domestic and foreign affairs.

Government programs and initiatives also play a role in promoting a national identity. Government organizations, such as the Canadian Radio-television and Telecommunications Commission (CRTC), the National Film Board, and Telefilm Canada, help to promote and fund Canadian media. Through Canadian media, Canadians are exposed to Canadian talent, issues, and culture, which better enables people to develop a sense of nationhood. In addition, the Department of Canadian Heritage works to strengthen connections among Canadians through the promotion of Canadian culture and traditions. This department provides funding for some local heritage festivals that celebrate Canada's multiculturalism while bringing people from different backgrounds together. It also promotes art and sport in Canada and works to promote national identity among Canada's youth by sponsoring initiatives such as the "Celebrate Canada!" poster challenge and exchange programs that allow youth in Canada to experience life through the eyes of Canadians in different regions of the country.

With policies like the one described in the following quotation, written media helps strengthen a sense
of Canadian identity. Magazines are required to be published with Canadian content and identity in mind, and Canadian writers are promoted as well.

PRACTICE QUESTIONS

Use the following information to answer the next question.

According to Statistics Canada, Canada's gross national product (total dollar value of goods and services produced in the country in a one-year period) in 1929 was 6.1 billion dollars, and in 1932, it was 3.8 billion dollars.

1. Which of the following statements is **most likely false** about the time from 1929 to 1932?

   A. A lot of Canadians were without work.

   B. Many companies were going out of business.

   C. Many people were not able to support their families.

   D. A lot of people chose to save money rather than spend.

2. There is not an even distribution of wealth and economic activity in the different Canadian provinces. Which province's economy suffered the **most** in the 1930s but now has a robust economy?

   A. Quebec

   B. Ontario

   C. Saskatchewan

   D. British Columbia

3. List the three new political parties that developed in the 1930s as possible solutions for the struggling Canadian economy.

   _____

   _____

   _____

   _____

4. Describe the following factors as causes for the growth and diversification of the Canadian economy following the Second World War.
   • Baby boom
   • Advertising
   • Increased immigration

   _____

   _____

   _____

   _____

5. Describe some of the positive aspects of American involvement in the Canadian economy.

_____

_____

_____

_____

Use the following information to answer the next question.

Historically, there have always been far more artists from the United States performing in Canada than Canadian artists. Here are some of the reasons:

- The cost of touring in a country with vast distances between cities is high.
- There is an extensive monopoly of concert productions by American agencies.
- There is a lack of Canadian artists working with American agencies.
- Young Canadian artists found it very difficult financially to break into the concert circuit.
- Government support of the arts was very low in Canada in the past.
- The idea of using public funds to support the arts was not favoured politically.

6. In order to reduce American participation in the Canadian entertainment industry, the **best** solution is to

A. increase government support for the arts

B. send more Canadian entertainers to the United States

C. disallow American entertainers from coming to Canada to tour

D. force the railways and airlines to subsidize entertainers' travel costs

Use the following information to answer the next question.

Factors That Have Affected the Quebec Economy Since 1960

Factors that have resulted in an increase in income	Factors that have resulted in economic cost
• Decline in birth rates	• Francization of Quebec society
• Growth of women in the labour force	• Threat of separation
• Rising educational standards	• The migration out of the province of a large portion of the old Anglophone business elite
• Francophone business class	• Decline of Montreal as a business centre

7. Explain the reason for Quebec's economic inequality with provinces such as Ontario and Alberta.

_____

_____

_____

_____

8. Which of the following people became successful in Canada in the production and sale of foods?

   A. K. C. Irving

   B. George Weston

   C. Heather Reisman

   D. Samuel Bronfman

9. Which of the following statements about Quebecor is **true**?

   A. Its focus is mostly on resources.

   B. It is a privately owned corporation.

   C. It is a successful government-run business.

   D. It is a successful business involving the government and the private sector.

10. Describe what former prime minister R. B. Bennett did to alleviate the problems of the Great Depression. What was his biggest mistake?

_____

_____

_____

_____

11. Human rights were restricted during the Second World War by

   A. forcing people to change jobs so that only weapons were being produced

   B. jailing citizens who voiced opposition to Canadian policies

   C. not allowing Aboriginal Canadians to serve in the military

   D. placing Japanese Canadians in internment camps

12. Which of the following statements regarding the reaction to the relocation of the Japanese Canadians and the denial of their rights is **correct**?

   A. Compensation was awarded in the 1980s.

   B. They were given their homes back after the Second World War.

   C. Prime Minister Mackenzie King issued an apology in 1945 after the war ended.

   D. An apology was given when the Charter of Rights and Freedoms was issued in 1982.

13. The first social program Canadians received was
    A. Medicare
    B. baby bonuses
    C. old age pensions
    D. unemployment insurance

14. Describe the pros and cons of Canada's social programs in contrast to the United States' social programs.

    _____
    _____
    _____
    _____

15. Describe two of the following actions that the government uses to make Canada a better place in which to live.
    • Ensuring the infrastructure is in good repair
    • Providing social programs to assist people in times of need
    • Sharing the costs of facilities for international athletic competitions

    _____
    _____
    _____
    _____
    _____

ANSWERS AND SOLUTIONS FOR PRACTICE QUESTIONS

1. D	5. OR	9. B	13. D
2. C	6. A	10. OR	14. OR
3. OR	7. OR	11. D	15. OR
4. OR	8. B	12. A	

1. D

The gross national product (GNP) is a measure of a country's productivity. It is least likely that people chose to save money rather than spend because the little, if any, money they had available was needed to purchase day-to-day necessities.

The decrease in the GNP reflects several factors, such as high unemployment rates and consumers with little money to spend. A lot of companies were forced out of business because they were not able to sell enough of their product.

2. C

While all the provinces in Canada suffered in the 1930s, the hardest hit was Saskatchewan. Because Saskatchewan relied primarily on farming, the province was hit not just by reduced demand, but also natural phenomena such as drought, dust storms, and grasshoppers. In the 1950s, demand for uranium helped diversify the Saskatchewan economy, and in the 1990s, demand for Saskatchewan's oil and gas turned it into a province with a strong economy.

3. Open Response

At least three new political parties—the Co-operative Commonwealth Federation in Saskatchewan, the Social Credit party in Alberta, and the Union Nationale in Quebec—emerged in the 1930s, all with possible solutions to the economic difficulties.

4. Open Response

Following the Second World War in 1945 and for the next 20 years, Canada's birth rate was well over 20 births per 1 000 people. This means at least 300 000 babies were born in 1945 to as high as 479 000 babies born in 1959. This baby boom led to increased demand for all kinds of different products.

Advertising in the 1950s contributed to a desire to spend money on the latest and newest products and fashions.

More immigrants were taken in after the war, adding to the demand for goods.

5. Open Response

American involvement in the Canadian economy has several positive outcomes. For example, it makes it easier to reach agreements on joint international projects (e.g., the St. Lawrence Seaway). At times, American entrepreneurs seem willing to take risks that Canadian entrepreneurs seem unwilling to take, not only creating jobs in Canada but modernizing industry as well. The trade agreements between Canada and the United States try to establish trade patterns that are economically beneficial for both countries.

6. **A**

The Massey Commission (the name applied to the Royal Commission on National Development in the Arts, Letters, and Sciences in the late 1940s and early 1950s) recommended that governments increase funding for aspiring artists. There were many obstacles to the Canadian entertainment industry related to the size of the country as well as the sheer volume of American-based talent that was able to record, tour, and perform in Canada.

7. **Open Response**

The continued threat of separation is an issue that has left some investors reluctant to invest in Quebec, meaning Quebec is still behind the "have" provinces. Prior to the Quiet Revolution of the 1960s, the gap between "have-not" Quebec and the "have" provinces was quite large. The gap has lessened because the decline in birth rates gives families more disposable income, rising educational standards prepare the labour force for better jobs, and the Francophone business class has contributed to the increase in living standards.

8. **B**

George Weston became successful in the food industry.

K. C. Irving was successful in the oil industry. Heather Reisman founded Indigo books, and Samuel Bronfman founded a liquor distilling company.

9. **B**

Quebecor is a private corporation that focuses on cable and telecommunications.

10. **Open Response**

When Bennett became prime minister in 1930, he tried to help end the depression by providing money for the unemployed to the provinces. He also tried to assist farmers by having the government pay part of the cost of transporting grain, and he lowered income tax.

R. B. Bennett did not follow the advice of economist John Maynard Keynes, who suggested increased government spending to the point of creating deficits and debts to be paid back when prosperity returned.

11. **D**

In 1942, Japanese Canadians had their property seized and were relocated to internment (detention) camps.

During the Second World War, freedom of speech was allowed unless it gave vital information to the enemy. Aboriginals could serve in the military, but had a hard time being accepted. Products were rationed because of shortages

12. **A**

The internment of the Japanese during the Second World War was not addressed until 1988. At this time, the Progressive Conservative government of Prime Minister Brian Mulroney acknowledged that the treatment was unjust, and surviving family members were given $21 000 each.

13. **D**

Although some Canadian provinces administered old age pensions (e.g., Manitoba in 1916), the unemployment insurance program of 1940 was the first federal social program.

Baby bonuses came a few years later, and it was not until the 1960s that the federal government introduced Medicare and old age pensions.

14. Open Response

Opponents of Canada's social programs might argue that some people will abuse the system, that it creates lazy, unmotivated people, and that it means higher taxes for everyone. Every Canadian benefits in some way from social programs, particularly health care, and the other social program "safety nets" are usually utilized by people who genuinely need the help.

The fact is that social programs do mean higher taxes for Canadians than for Americans, whose social programs are not as comprehensive; however, there are expenses in the United States, such as private health-care insurance, that could easily eat up much of the tax savings.

15. Open Response

All levels of government take care of different parts of the infrastructure, making Canada an easy and safe country in which to live, work, and travel. As well, all levels of government have been involved in the building of sports facilities, so Canadian cities can host events such as the Olympic Games, the Commonwealth Games, and several other international sporting events that attract tourists. There are social programs available to help Canadians when they are out of work, for example, and health-care coverage for all Canadians.

UNIT TEST

Use the following information to answer the next question.

Speaker I	Voting for our party will result in more money being spent on old age pensions, child care, and unemployment, but will also possibly result in higher taxes.
Speaker II	Our goal is to ensure that Canadians can make choices as to what they want to do with their money. Most Canadians want to rely on themselves.
Speaker III	We will try to help where and when it is necessary; however, we do not want to over-tax the citizens.
Speaker IV	The entire system is broken; the wealthy take advantage of everybody. The solution is to have the government own everything and distribute wealth equally.

1. Which speaker **best** reflects the goals of Canada's New Democratic Party?

   A. Speaker I

   B. Speaker II

   C. Speaker III

   D. Speaker IV

2. Describe economic life in Canada after the Second World War.

   _____

   _____

   _____

   _____

Use the following information to answer the next question.

Speaker I	American investors are taking advantage of us; all the profits go to the United States.
Speaker II	American investments have created a lot of jobs for Canadians.
Speaker III	Sooner or later, the Americans will gain control of our economy. Political control is next.
Speaker IV	Some of these industries would not get off the ground if we waited for Canadians to come up with the money.

3. Which speakers favour continued American investment in the Canadian economy?

   A. Speakers I and III

   B. Speakers II and III

   C. Speakers II and IV

   D. Speakers III and IV

4. Briefly describe the lows and highs of Saskatchewan's economy from the 1930s through to today.

_____

_____

_____

_____

Use the following information to answer the next question.

A student researching a famous Canadian came up with the following information:

- Born in Austria in 1932
- Started first business in 1957
- Involved in thoroughbred horse racing
- Value of business said to be $20 billion

5. Who is the person being researched?
   A. K. C. Irving

   B. Frank Stronach

   C. George Weston

   D. Samuel Bronfman

6. Describe some of the actions that the Canadian government took during the Great Depression to help people in need.

_____

_____

_____

_____

7. Write a paragraph describing Canada's treatment of Japanese people in Canada during the Second World War.

_____

_____

_____

_____

Read the following letter to the editor and answer the next question.

Dear Editor:

Since it was introduced in Saskatchewan in the 1940s and became a federal program in the 1960s, taxes have been going up. People should not be relying on the government—it is everybody's own responsibility to ensure that their basic needs are being taken care of. There are a lot of jobs in this country; Canadians need to work harder and save for emergencies. Canada's public education system is second to none, and everybody has the opportunity to learn the skills to make a living. It is true that there are some people who have physical and mental challenges and cannot succeed; they are entitled to public assistance. However, most Canadians can take care of themselves, especially if tax rates are lower.

Sincerely,
Name Withheld

8. The writer of this letter is **most** critical about
   A. unemployment and employment insurance
   B. family allowance and the child tax benefit
   C. the Canada Pension Plan
   D. the Canada Health Act

9. Which of the following events happened in Canada during both World Wars?
   A. Compulsory military service
   B. An increase in unemployment
   C. Internment of Japanese and other Asians
   D. An increase in the availability of consumer goods

10. Explain why the universal family allowance was replaced in the 1990s with the non-universal Child Tax Credit.

   _____

   _____

   _____

   _____

ANSWERS AND SOLUTIONS FOR UNIT TEST

1. A	4. OR	7. OR	10. OR
2. OR	5. B	8. D	
3. C	6. OR	9. A	

1. A

Speaker I reflects the views of the New Democratic Party. They want to keep most production in private hands but provide more social programs.

Speaker II most likely reflects the views of the Conservative party, Speaker III most likely reflects the views of the Liberal party, and Speaker IV most likely reflects the views of the Communist party.

2. Open Response

Following the Second World War, the Canadian economy became very prosperous. The government took an active role in looking after war veterans and creating a social safety net, which included unemployment benefits and baby bonuses. As well, many new consumer goods based on new technology appeared on the market.

3. C

Speakers II and IV point out the advantages of job creation and the development of industry.

Speakers I and III make statements that oppose American investment on the basis of economic nationalism.

4. Open Response

In Saskatchewan in the 1930s, agriculture was the main economic activity, so people in Saskatchewan were extremely hard hit by the Great Depression. By the 1990s, the economy was more diverse, including potash, uranium, oil, and gas, leading to greater economic stability and growth in the province.

5. B

Frank Stronach is the person that the student is researching.

Samuel Bronfman was in the liquor distillery business, George Weston was in food production, and K. C. Irving was in the oil industry.

6. Open Response

During the Depression, municipalities ran soup kitchens and provided some relief money to buy necessities. Also in 1931, Prime Minister Bennett subsidized freight rates so farmers could transport their grain.

7. Open Response

The Canadian government used the War Measures Act to strip Japanese residents—75% were Canadian citizens—of their rights and place them in internment camps. Over 21 000 Japanese people lived in British Columbia and were sent to towns in the Rockies. Their possessions, including their houses, were taken away. Their rights were given back in 1949, and there was an official government apology given in 1988.

8. D

The writer of this letter does not agree that Canadians should have a publically funded health-care system. While the writer may also disagree with other social welfare programs, the clues to determining what the writer is talking about are that it was introduced in Saskatchewan in the 1940s and it became a federal program in the 1960s.

9. A

Conscription, or compulsory military service, was necessary during both World Wars.

During the Second World War, unemployment levels dropped to extremely low levels and more than one million women joined the workforce. The Japanese were interned during the Second World War. There was a decreased availability of consumer goods during the wars.

10. Open Response

In the late 1980s and early 1990s, government debt kept growing, and paying the interest on a growing debt was using up too much of the revenues that the government had. Decisions were made to reduce spending on some programs, such as family allowance, by changing the focus from universal to individual needs.

Class Focus
Methods of Historical Inquiry & Communication

METHODS OF HISTORICAL INQUIRY AND COMMUNICATION

This section of the KEY can be used throughout the year and with any concept you are learning in class. Methods of historical inquiry and communication provide you with strategies to determine the validity of information about a topic or event, to analyze issues and problems from the past by placing people and events in context, and to reflect on perspectives and opinions based on information you have gathered and researched.

5.1.5 organize and record information gathered through research

RESEARCH

Let's say you are asked to research a specific topic. You need to find ideas and information related to that topic. These will make up the substance, or main body, of your research. By using some or all of the following steps and strategies, you will be able to keep your research manageable, find reliable resources, and acknowledge the experts and writers who provided you with your information.

CREATE A RESEARCH PLAN

The following is an example of a checklist-style plan that can help you stay focused and on track:

1. Topic chosen: _____
2. Assignment expectations: _____
3. KWL chart created
4. Webbing for preliminary ideas

Example

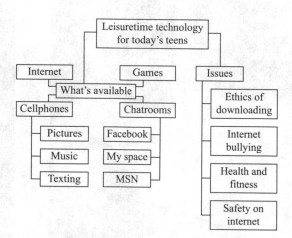

5. Topic restated as a question
6. Available information listed; i.e., a preview of readily available resources, people you could interview, etc.
7. Preliminary research conclusion; i.e., does my topic need to be adjusted so that it fits available resources?
8. Further questions related to the topic _____
9. Data collected and point-form notes completed
10. Source information recorded for bibliography
11. Information organized and outline drafted

12. Rough draft of paper completed
13. Good copy of paper completed
14. Bibliography added
15. Title page and table of contents added

Sticking to these steps will ensure that your writing will be the best that it can be on the day the assignment is due.

Record Information

Keeping your information organized helps you to:

- find and use the information later
- ensure that you never plagiarize
- separate quotations and sources of quotations from other information

While keeping a record of your research and the information you collect is important, any method you use to do this is fine. For example, you could use index cards to record your information, possibly in point form with one source per index card.

To organize your information, you could make practical topic headings on the cards, such as "Quotations" or "References." As long as you have a written record of your information, computer documents or spreadsheets, notebooks, or index cards are all fine places to keep track of your sources.

5.1.4   evaluate the credibility of sources and information

CHECKING RELIABILITY

How do you decide whether or not to believe what you read? Can you tell fact from opinion? How do you know whether or not you can trust the writer?

Factual statements are clear, accurate, and verifiable. Unfortunately, some of what you read may not be factual even though it appears to be true or others whom you trust say that it is true. Magazines, books, newspapers, websites, bulletin boards, and blogs, for example, should not be trusted until the writer's knowledge and experience on the subject has been verified. Faulty conclusions can be made when the evidence provided contains incorrect observations or statements that are prejudiced, wishful, or imaginative.

Try examining a piece of writing from the following angles in order to determine how credible it is:

Writer's viewpoint: Who is the writer? What does he or she stand to gain or lose? An article about politics may be very biased if it is written, for example, by the leader of a political party.

Text structure: Is the information presented well? Are the arguments easy to understand, logical, and supported by reasonable evidence? Sloppy work may indicate that the work has not been reviewed carefully and is not credible.

Writer's word choice: Do the writer's words express ideas and convey facts, or are they meant to inflame readers' emotions? Does the tone of the writer seem balanced or angry?

FINAL TIPS ON RELIABILITY AND ACCURACY

- Compare facts using various resources, and watch for differences or contradictions.
- Consider the publishing date. Is the information current?
- Consider the expertise and reputation of the source.
- Watch for biases. Is the information objective, or does it favour/criticize a particular group?
- Double-check Internet sources. Is there information about the writer's expertise? Is the site reliable overall? How recent is the information on the website? Is the website educational or commercial in nature?
- Double-check your own accuracy. Make sure your information is valid before doing a final print of your assignment.

5.1.3   distinguish between primary and secondary sources of information and use both in historical research

PRIMARY AND SECONDARY SOURCES

Both primary and secondary sources are important elements of research. They often determine the degree of accuracy and reliability of information. Research articles with a variety of sources usually can be taken more seriously than research articles with few sources.

The following chart gives examples of both primary and secondary sources:

Primary Source	Secondary Source
Autobiography	Biography
Interview with a Titanic survivor	News story written after the Titanic sank
Original manuscript of a book	Translated or revised edition of a book

Interviews can be either primary or secondary sources of information. For example, if you were doing a research paper on the Quebec ice storm, a primary source interview would be with a person who lived through the disaster. A secondary source interview would be with a professor who studies the impact of disasters on regions in Canada. Both primary and secondary source interviews are an excellent means of gathering information you might not find in a book.

Searching

You can search in your library catalogue for materials that are related to your topic by typing in any piece of information from the list below:

- title
- keyword
- author
- subject
- call number
- series title
- ISBN/ISSN: This is a cataloguing number found at the bottom of the credits page, and it looks like this: 0-03-052664-7
  (These numbers represent a text entitled *Elements of Language: Second Course*)

Your catalogue search could produce titles and call numbers for several books on your topic, and you can take that information with you to your local library.

At the Library

When you go to a library, the librarian can help you find the information you are looking for. Most libraries are divided into sections to help people easily locate materials. Some sections that the librarian might show you include:

- reference materials (dictionaries, encyclopedias, atlases). Usually, these books may only be used in the library.
- audio/visual (movies, music, games)
- periodicals (newspapers, magazines, journals)
- non-fiction books

All library books are classified or grouped according to one of two systems: the Dewey Decimal System or the Library of Congress Classification (LCC). Most Canadian and American libraries use the Dewey Decimal System. Usually, only very large libraries use the Library of Congress Classification.

With these classification systems, each book has a specific code that determines where it can be found in the library. The following tables show how these two systems organize non-fiction books by number or letter.

Dewey Decimal System	
000	General works
100	Philosophy
200	Religion
300	Social sciences
400	Language
500	Science
600	Technology
700	Fine arts
800	Literature
900	History and geography

Library of Congress System	
A	General works
B	Philosophy, psychology, religion
C	History and related sciences
D	History: general and Old World
E–F	History: the Americas
G	Geography, anthropology, recreation
H	Social sciences
J	Political science
K	Law
L	Education
M	Music
N	Fine arts
P	Language and literature
Q	Science
R	Medicine
S	Agriculture
T	Technology
U	Military science
V	Naval science
Z	Bibliography and library science

The following chart explains the Dewey Decimal System classification for a book called *The Biology of the Honey Bee*, by Mark L. Winston.

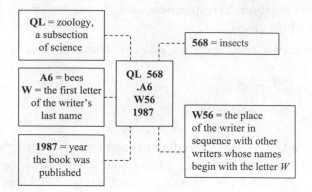

To find this book in the library, look in numerical order in the QL section for 568. Then, look in alphabetical order in the books under QL568 for A6. Finally, look at the books under QL568.A6 for W56.

Online Searches

Online searches involve using keywords and phrases to research your topic on the Internet. Be as specific as possible when searching. For example, the keywords "provincial election in Ontario" will yield more applicable results than the keywords "provincial election." Sometimes, you have to try a few different keywords or phrases before you find sites that match what you are trying to research. When you find an article related to your topic, watch for hyperlinks to other related articles or websites.

The sites that are listed first in an online search vary depending on which search engine you are using. Usually, the websites listed on the first page of your search results will be the most relevant, but this is not always the case. Some search engines index sites by number of hits or by number of links to a site. Sometimes, the owners of websites will pay to be ranked on the first page of a search. Play around with keywords and phrases. Often, if you see the same sites more than once, those sites are likely to be relevant.

Information from the Internet is like any other kind of published information. Make sure to cite the information in your bibliography if you use any material from an online source.

Dictionaries and Encyclopedias

Dictionaries and encyclopedias are among the most useful reference materials in the library. Both dictionaries and encyclopedias can be particularly helpful when you are starting a research project and want basic information.

If you do not understand what your topic means, dictionaries are the best place to find the definitions of words. When a word has more than one definition, look for the meaning of the word associated with your specific subject or content area. For instance, the word *revolution* is used in both science and social studies, but the word has two totally different meanings.

Example

rev•o•lu•tion (rev′ə lōō′shən), n. **1.** the
overthrow and replacement of an established
government or political system by
the people governed. **2.** a sudden, complete,
or radical change. **3.** rotation on or
as if on an axis. **4.** the orbiting of one
celestial body around another. **5.** a single
cycle in a rotation or orbit. **–rev′o•lu′•tion•ary′**,
 adj., n., pl **–ies. –rev′o•lu′•tion•ist**, *n.*

Encyclopedias are reliable sources of basic information about a large number of topics. Most libraries do not allow you to check out encyclopedias, so, you will have to use them for your research in the library. Remember that libraries also have electronic encyclopedias on CD-ROMs. The advantage of electronic encyclopedias is that the information is updated regularly, as needed. You can also access all major encyclopedias, such as *Encyclopaedia Britannia Online*, from your computer. This is much cheaper than purchasing a printed set of encyclopedias.

CD-ROMs on many subjects and topics are available through your library. If you want to cite a CD-ROM for a research paper, the following example shows how it would appear in a bibliography:

> "Title of Article." *Title of Database.* Medium (CD-ROM). Electronic Publisher,
> publication date.

Example

> "Technology." *Encyclopaedia Britannica.* CD-ROM. Encyclopaedia Britannica, Inc., 2008.

INTERVIEWING EXPERTS

Interviews with experts or community members can also yield excellent information. Interviews are especially useful if you are researching something that is very current. Chances are there will be little printed or online information on a very new topic or event in your topic area. In this situation, an interview might be the best resource for getting up-to-date information.

5.3.2   use an accepted form of documentation to acknowledge all sources of information, including electronic sources

BIBLIOGRAPHIES

In order to create a complete and correct bibliography, you need to record certain information for all sources used in your research, including the name of the author, the title, the publisher, any website information, the place of publication, and the volume number.

Always follow the guidelines for creating a bibliography laid out by your teacher. The following formats are examples of how to record source information for references used in your research.

Book

Author. *Title*. City: Publisher, Year.

Example

McCrae, Andrew. *Teens and Their Culture*.
Boston: Boston University Press, 2006.

Periodical (magazine, newspaper)

Author. "Title of Article." *Publication Name*, Date.

Example

Brolin, Megan. "Online Predators." *Teen by Teen News*, May 7, 2007.

Encyclopedia

"Name of Article." *Title of Book*, Edition number. Publisher, Date.

Example

"Technology." *Encyclopaedia Britannica*, 15th ed. Encyclopaedia Britannica, Inc., 2007.

Electronic Sources

Author (if known). "Document Title." Website or Database Title. Date of electronic publication. Name of Sponsoring Institution. Date information was accessed. <URL>

"Internet Safety Network for Teens." Parent Share. July 2006. Ontario Association of Children's Aid Societies. Nov 2007. <http://www.occas.org/childwelfare/links.htm>

Information Sources

You can access online library catalogues by typing the name of your local library into an Internet search (Toronto Public Library, Burlington Public Library, or Thunder Bay Public Library, for example). When you perform this search, you will find links to:

- library catalogues
- databases by subject or title
- frequently asked questions, such as "How do I use the library catalogue?"

5.1.1   formulate different types of questions when researching historical topics, issues and events

QUESTIONS TO GUIDE YOUR INQUIRY

Once you have chosen a topic, try to think of some questions that will help you to focus or direct your inquiry. For instance, if you chose the topic "The Element of Surprise at Pearl Harbor," you might ask the following questions:

- In what way did the Japanese launch a surprise attack on Pearl Harbor?
- Where in Pearl Harbor did they attack?
- How did the Americans respond to the attack?
- What did the Americans learn from this event?
- Did the Japanese successfully complete any other surprise attacks during World War II? If so, where?
- How did the Americans use the element of surprise to turn the tables on the Japanese?

To keep your research focused and effective, you need to evaluate your questions. You may choose to eliminate some questions that are not relevant enough to your specific topic, such as the last two questions from the above list.

You may wish to arrange the questions in a logical order to help organize the information for your paper. Often, key questions can be used as sub-topics. For example, if your main topic is "Where in Pearl Harbor did the Japanese attack?" a subheading for your paper could be "Attack Targets."

Identifying Key Words and Phrases

The topic and inquiry questions you generate can provide a great starting point for your research. As you begin to find books and Internet articles on your topic, watch for keywords and phrases that will lead to more in-depth information. For example, some keywords and phrases that would help with Pearl Harbor research might include:

- Hickam Air Force Base
- Bellows Air Force Station
- Wheeler Army Airfield
- Casualties at Pearl Harbor
- United States Intelligence Pearl Harbor
- Surprise attack on Pearl Harbor
- Aftermath of Pearl Harbor
- Warnings before attack on Pearl Harbor

Stay organized about key terms and phrases to ensure that you do not forget to include some part of your assignment.

Organizing information helps you at several stages in the writing process. Staying organized while forming ideas at the developing stage of an assignment helps you narrow down or fine-tune what you want to write about. It also gives you a sense of the information you will be able to use in the assignment. You can keep tabs on what information you want to use and what you might eventually like to leave out.

Being organized will help you develop clearly formed ideas and effectively get those ideas across to your reader. Use the methods that work best for you. Time spent organizing before you sit down to write will save you a lot of time in the long run and will ensure that you create the best writing possible.

5.2.4 draw conclusions on the basis of relevant and sufficient supporting evidence

FACT AND OPINION

Factual statements are ones that can be proven to be true. Experiments, research, or observations can provide proof that factual statements are true. Opinions are statements that express personal beliefs. They are not always based on facts and cannot always be proven to be true. Sometimes, it is difficult to tell the difference between a fact and an opinion; other times, it is very obvious. As the reader, you must try to separate the two.

NOTE: The above two paragraphs are almost identical to the second paragraph in the section "Checking Reliability." Please see that edited version if you would like it repeated here.

Not everything that is stated with authority is really a fact. Almanacs, encyclopedias, and atlases are examples of reference materials that are usually reliable sources of factual information. Other resources, such as eyewitness accounts, newspaper accounts, and supermarket tabloid accounts are often less reliable. Information on the Internet often has errors or bias.

How do you determine what makes a resource reliable as a source of information? When is the information valid and authentic? What kinds of sources will provide the most accurate information?

It is important to be critical of what you read, particularly when the information you are reading claims to be factual or truthful. Evaluate the stated facts carefully. Decide what evidence is convincing and what might need verification. Look for viewpoints or opinions that suggest a particular bias, even when the bias is not directly stated. For example, if a newspaper prints stories and articles that cast a particular politician or political party only in a negative light, you could probably reach the conclusion that the paper does not support the policies of that politician or party. It is a good idea either not to read a newspaper that has a bias, or to balance your knowledge of issues by reading a variety of news sources.

5.2.1 analyse information, employing concepts and approaches appropriate to historical inquiry

LOCATING AND RECALLING INFORMATION

As you read, you need to remember the points of a story or an article in order to understand them. Information is often structured in terms of *idea and example*, *cause and effect*, or *chronological sequence*. You will find that you regularly see combinations of these concepts.

Idea and Example

An idea-and-example structure is one in which an idea is presented and then followed by specific evidence, as shown in the following paragraph from "Poisonous Spiders."

<u>There are about 6 different species of black widow spiders.</u> → Topic (idea) is black widow spiders

<u>Three of these species are found in the warm southern United States</u>. Black widow spiders build webs, and they live wherever they can build one. They rarely live in houses and other buildings, but if the weather gets very cold, they can move inside. Black widow spiders eat insects, and stay in their webs to catch them. Only the female black widow spider is dangerous. She is considered to be the most venomous spider in the United States! Females are shiny black, with a red hourglass shaped mark on the bottom of their abdomens. Although they are dangerous, black widow spiders are not usually deadly because they only inject a very small amount of poison. → The rest of the paragraph presents specific information about black widow spiders

Cause and Effect

Sometimes writers use cause and effect to explain why something happens and why things are as they are. Cause and effect is often used in writing that informs, explains, or persuades. Such writing includes cause-and-effect words such as *because, as a result, why, when, therefore, so, for this reason*, and *if...then*.

A cause-and-effect structure shows how one event determines a specific outcome. In the following passage, a cause-and-effect structure is used to describe how the bubonic plague spread.

THE BLACK DEATH: BUBONIC PLAGUE

In the early 1330s, an outbreak of deadly bubonic plague occurred in China. The bubonic plague mainly affects rodents, but fleas can transmit the disease to people. Once people are infected, they infect others very rapidly. Plague causes fever and a painful swelling of the lymph glands called buboes, which is how it gets its name. The disease also causes spots on the skin that are red at first and then turn black.

Since China was one of the busiest of the world's trading nations, it was only a matter of time before the outbreak of plague in China spread to western Asia and Europe. In October of 1347, several Italian merchant ships returned from a trip to the Black Sea, one of the key links in trade with China. When the ships docked in Sicily, many of those on board were already dying of plague. Within days, the disease spread to the city and the surrounding countryside.

Cause	Effect
Bubonic plague develops in Chinese rodents.	Fleas transfer the disease to people.
Infected people transmit the bubonic plague.	Fever, "buboes" (swollen glands), and spots on the skin are some plague symptoms.
China is a large trading nation.	Plague spreads to western Asia and Europe.
In 1347, ships from China arrive in Sicily.	Disease spreads from the ships' crews and passengers to Sicilians.
The disease spreads quickly all across Europe.	About one-third of Europe's population dies of plague.

Chronological Sequence

Sometimes it is helpful to keep track of information in terms of the sequence of time. If you look for a logical time ordering (chronology) while reading, you may find it easier to locate and recall details. For example, if you wanted to name the last five premiers of Ontario, you could list them in chronological order as shown:

David Peterson	1985–1990
Bob Rae	1990–1995
Mike Harris	1995–2002
Ernie Eves	2002–2003
Dalton McGuinty	2003–present

Chronological order refers to what happened or what is happening over a certain time period. Writers organize and present their ideas chronologically when they want to present a series of events or steps in the order in which they occurred.

The article "The Black Death: Bubonic Plague" presents its ideas in chronological order, making the sequence of events—included in the table following this article—easy to follow.

THE BLACK DEATH: BUBONIC PLAGUE

In the early 1330s, an outbreak of deadly bubonic plague occurred in China. The bubonic plague mainly affects rodents, but fleas can transmit the disease to people. Once people are infected, they infect others very rapidly. Plague causes fever and a painful swelling of the lymph glands called buboes, which is how it gets its name. The disease also causes spots on the skin that are red at first and then turn black.

Since China was one of the busiest of the world's trading nations, it was only a matter of time before the outbreak of plague in China spread to western Asia and Europe. In October of 1347, several Italian merchant ships returned from a trip to the Black Sea, one of the key links in trade with China. When the ships docked in Sicily, many of those on board were already dying of plague. Within days, the disease spread to the city and the surrounding countryside. An eyewitness tells what happened:

"Realizing what a deadly disaster had come to them, the people quickly drove the Italians from their city. But the disease remained, and soon death was everywhere. Fathers abandoned their sick sons. Lawyers refused to come and make out wills for the dying. Friars and nuns were left to care for the sick, and monasteries and convents were soon deserted, as they were stricken, too. Bodies were left in empty houses, and there was no one to give them a Christian burial."

The disease struck and killed people with terrible speed. The Italian writer Boccaccio said its victims often "ate lunch with their friends and dinner with their ancestors in paradise."

By the following August, the plague had spread as far north as England, where people called it "The Black Death" because of the black spots it produced on the skin. A terrible killer was loose across Europe, and medieval medicine had nothing to combat it.

In winter, the disease seemed to disappear, but only because fleas—which were now helping to carry it from person to person—are dormant then. Each spring, the plague attacked again, killing new victims. After five years, 25 million people were dead—one-third of Europe's people.

Even when the worst was over, smaller outbreaks continued, not just for years, but for centuries. The survivors lived in constant fear of the plague's return, and the disease did not disappear until the 1600s.

Medieval society never recovered from the results of the plague. So many people had died that there were serious labour shortages all over Europe. This led workers to demand higher wages, but landlords refused those demands. By the end of the 1300s, peasant revolt broke out in England, France, Belgium, and Italy.

The disease took its toll on the church as well. People throughout Christendom had prayed devoutly for deliverance from the plague. Why hadn't those prayers been answered? A new period of political turmoil and philosophical questioning lay ahead.

Chronological Sequence

Year	Event
Early 1330s	Outbreak of bubonic plague in China
1347	Italian ships brought plague to Europe from China
1348	Plague reached England
By 1352	25 million Europeans had died
1352–1600s	Small outbreaks of plague continued
1600s	Plague finally disappeared

5.2.3   identify different viewpoints and explicit biases when interpreting information for a research project or when participating in a discussion

ASSESSING BOTH SIDES OF AN ISSUE

In order to become a skilled debater on any issue, it is an excellent strategy to be well prepared to argue or defend either side of an argument. Exploring both sides of an issue also helps you to understand opinions that may differ from your own. You will become more confident and comfortable with your own viewpoint if you can support it with evidence.

People have differing views of whether zoos are moral, for example. The following graphic organizer presents both sides of the controversial issue. Some people are strongly opposed to the very idea of animals being held in captivity so that people can watch them for money. Others think zoos are an acceptable source of entertainment and education. Who is right? After looking at the supporting arguments for both sides, notice that the conclusion provided turns out to be somewhat of a compromise between the two opposing viewpoints. This often happens in real debates and is an ideal approach to respecting different opinions.

Supporting Arguments		Opposing Arguments
Help educate people about different animals in their area		Animals show signs of stress, boredom, and unhappiness
Protect endangered animals		Animals belong in their natural habitats
Provide scientists with a place to study animals up close		Some animals are abused in captivity
Provide veterinarians and zoologists with a place to learn about caring for wild animals	**Should there be zoos?**	Scientists would learn more by studying animals in the wild
Help injured animals that could not survive in the wild		The natural world is for the survival of the fittest; humans should not interfere
Make money that can pay for animal care in the wild		Humans do not have the right to capture animals
Zoos, wildlife preserves, and aquariums may be the only place for some people to see wild animals and learn about them		Animals are forced to entertain. Parks make lots of money that is not all used for animal welfare

Conclusion
Zoos could be created so that the animals can live in conditions similar to their natural habitats with minimal interference from people. Wildlife preserves help protect animals from the expansion of towns and cities. These preserves can provide a safe haven for migrating birds and animals.

Reasons
• The welfare of the animals is important; they do not choose to be in a zoo. • People sometimes cause problems for animals in the wild by invading their habitats. • Zoos can help educate people about the importance of protecting wildlife and living in harmony with animals. People should not destroy animals' homes or kill for fun or body parts. • Videos can be used to show animals in their natural world. Thus people do not have to capture animals and put them on display.

Biases

Bias is an unconscious or natural tendency to favour a particular thing. It may be unspoken, but it is often expressed in attitude or behaviour. A bias certainly can be positive, such as a pro-Canada bias (having an inner pride in being Canadian) or a bias to cheer for your home team no matter what. However, there are negative biases, such as the following:

• *anti-youth bias*, which refers to assumptions made about young people, including misconceptions about the trustworthiness of youth

• *anti-aging bias*, which refers to assumptions made about older people, including misconceptions that they are obsolete because of their age

• *anti-authority bias*, which makes a person view teachers, parents, policemen, or other authority figures with hostility and suspicion

• *racial prejudice*, which makes a person dislike or hate anyone who looks different from their own ethnic group

Other biases include political biases, gender biases, economic biases, and religious biases.
Negative biases prevent people from being tolerant of others and of different viewpoints.

Key Strategies for Success on Tests

KEY STRATEGIES FOR SUCCESS ON TESTS

Having a good understanding of effective test-taking skills can help your performance on any test. Being familiar with question formats can help you in preparing for quizzes, unit tests or year-end assessments.

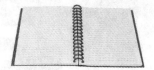

TEST PREPARATION AND TEST-TAKING SKILLS
THINGS TO CONSIDER WHEN TAKING A TEST

⤴ It is normal to feel anxious before writing a test. You can manage this anxiety by thinking positive thoughts. Visual imagery is a helpful technique to try. Make a conscious effort to relax by taking several slow, controlled, deep breaths. Concentrate on the air going in and out of the body.

⤴ Before you begin the test, ask questions if you are unsure of anything.

⤴ Jot down key words or phrases from any oral directions.

⤴ Look over the entire test to assess the number and kinds of questions on the test.

⤴ Read each question carefully and reread it if necessary.

⤴ Pay close attention to key vocabulary words. Sometimes these words are bolded or italicized, and they are usually important words in the question.

⤴ Mark your answers on your answer sheet carefully. If you wish to change an answer, erase the mark and then ensure that your final answer is darker than the one that you have erased.

⤴ On the test booklet, use highlighting to note directions, key words, and vocabulary that you find confusing or that are important to answering the question.

⤴ **Double-check** to make sure you have answered everything before handing in your test.

When taking tests, some words are often overlooked. Failure to pay close attention to these words can result in an incorrect answer. One way to avoid this is to be aware of these words and to <u>underline</u>, circle or **highlight** these words while you are taking the test.

Even though the following words are easy to understand, they are also easy to miss and can change the meaning of the question and/or answer significantly.

all	always	most likely	probably	best	not
difference	usually	except	most	unlikely	likely

Example

1. During the race, Susan is **most likely** feeling

   A. sad

   B. weak

   C. scared

   D. determined

HELPFUL STRATEGIES FOR ANSWERING MULTIPLE-CHOICE QUESTIONS

A multiple-choice question provides some information for you to consider and then asks you to select a response from four choices. There will be one correct answer. The other answers are distracters, which are incorrect.

Here are some strategies to help you when answering multiple-choice questions.

- Quickly skim through the entire test. Find out how many questions there are and plan your time accordingly.
- Read and reread questions carefully. Underline key words and try to think of an answer before looking at the choices.
- If there is a graphic, look at the graphic, read the question, and go back to the graphic. Then, you may want to circle the important information from the question.
- Carefully read the choices. Read the question first and then each answer with it.
- When choosing an answer, try to eliminate those choices that are clearly wrong or do not make sense.
- Some questions may ask you to select the best answer. These questions will always include words like **best, most strongly**, and **most clearly**. All of the answers will be correct to some degree, but one of the choices will be "best" in some way. Carefully read all four choices (A, B, C, D) before choosing the answer you think is the best.
- If you do not know the answer or if the question does not make sense to you, it is better to guess than to leave it blank.
- Do not spend too much time on any one question. Make a mark (*) beside a difficult question and come back to it. If you are leaving a question to come back to later, make sure that you also leave the space on the answer sheet.
- Remember to go back to the difficult questions at the end of the test; sometimes clues are given throughout the test that will provide you with answers.
- Note any negatives such as **no** or **not** and be sure your choice fits the question.
- Before changing an answer, **be sure** you have a very good reason to do so.
- Do not look for patterns on your answer sheet.

HELPFUL STRATEGIES FOR ANSWERING OPEN-RESPONSE QUESTIONS

An open-response question requires you to respond to a question or directive such as **explain, predict, list, describe, use information from the text and your own ideas; provide the main idea and supporting details**. In preparing for open-response tasks you may wish to:

- Read and re-read the question carefully.
- Recognize and pay close attention to **directing words** such as **explain, predict, and describe**.
- <u>Underline</u> key words and phrases that indicate what is required in your answer, such as <u>explain</u>, <u>summarize</u>, <u>mainly about</u>, <u>what is the meaning of</u>, <u>best shows</u>…
- Write down rough, point-form notes regarding the information you want to include in your answer.
- Think about what you want to say and organize information and ideas in a coherent and concise manner within the time limit you have for the question.
- Be sure to answer every part of the question that is asked.
- Stick to the question, be brief and only answer what is asked.
- Answer in full and correctly written sentences keeping your answer within the space provided.
- Re-read your response to ensure you have answered the question.
- **Think:** Does your answer make sense?
- **Listen:** Does it sound right?
- Use the appropriate subject vocabulary and terminology in your response.

TEST PREPARATION COUNTDOWN

If you develop a plan for studying and test preparation, you will perform well on tests.

Here is a general plan to follow seven days before you write a test.

Countdown: Seven Days Before the Test

1. Review important areas in which to gather information

   - areas to be included on the test
   - types of test items
   - general and specific test tips

2. Start preparing for the test at least seven days prior to the test-taking day. Develop your test preparation plan and set time aside to prepare and study.

Countdown: from Six to Two Days Before the Test

1. Review old homework assignments, quizzes, and tests.
2. Rework problems on quizzes and tests to make sure you still know how to solve them.
3. Correct any errors made on quizzes and tests.
4. Review key concepts, processes, formulas, and vocabulary.
5. Create practice test questions for yourself and then answer them. Work out lots of sample problems.

Countdown: The Night Before the Test

1. The night before the test is for final preparation, which includes reviewing and gathering material needed for the test before going to bed.
2. Most important is getting a good night's rest knowing that you have done everything within your means to do well on the test.

The Day of the Test

1. Eat a nutritious breakfast.
2. Ensure that you have all the necessary materials.
3. Think positive thoughts: "I can do this!" "I am ready!" "I know I can do well!"
4. Arrive at your school early so that you are not rushing. A stressful, rushed morning can set a hurried or anxious pace for the test.

SUCCESS TIPS DURING THE TEST

The following strategies can be useful to use when writing your test.

- Take two or three deep breaths to help you relax.
- Read the directions carefully and underline, circle, or highlight any key words.
- Survey the entire test to get a flavour of what you will need to do.
- Budget your time.
- Begin with an easy question or a question that you know you can answer correctly rather than following the numerical question order of the test.
- If you draw a blank on the test, try repeating the deep breathing and physical relaxation activities first. Then move to visualization and positive self-talk to get you going.
- Write down anything that you remember about the subject on the reverse side of your test paper. This activity sometimes helps you to remind yourself that you do know something and you are capable of writing the test.
- Look over your test when you have finished and double-check your answers to be sure you did not forget anything.

NOTES

TABLE OF CORRELATIONS				
Strand	**General Expectation**	**Specific Outcome**	**Practice Questions**	**Unit Test**
1 Communities: Local, national, and Global	1.1 describe some of the major local, national, and global forces and events that have influenced Canada's policies and Canadian identity since 1914	1.1.1 describe some of the policies championed by political leaders since 1914 that have contributed to a sense of Canadian identity	36	37
		1.1.2 identify the contributions made by selected regional, provincial, linguistic, ethnic, and/or religious communities to Canada's multicultural society	45	
		1.1.3 describe how Canada's participation in selected world events and contributions to international organizations and agreements have contributed to an evolving sense of national identity		
		1.1.4 identify some of the ways in which foreign power have influenced Canadian foreign policy		5, 7, 17
		1.1.5 describe some aspects of the impact in Canada of the experience and memory of the Holocaust	5	
		1.1.6 explain how American culture and lifestyles have influenced Canada and Canadians in selected periods		
	1.2 explain the significance of some key individuals and events in the evolution of French-English relations in Canada since 1914	1.2.1 explain why conscription was a controversial issue and how it divided English Canada and Quebec during the World War I and World War II	7	8
		1.2.2 identify some major events that contributed to the growth of Quebec nationalism and the separatist movement in Quebec from 1945	9	9
		1.2.3 describe key responses by Canadians and their political leaders to the Quebec separatist movement	8	10, 34
		1.2.4 identify the major groups of French Canadians outside Quebec and describe some of their efforts to achieve recognition		

		1.3.1 identify the causes of World War I and World War II and explain how Canada became involved in these two wars	10	11, 14
	1.3 evaluate Canada's participation in war and contributions to peacekeeping and security	1.3.2 describe some of the contributions Canada and Canadians made to the war effort overseas during World War I and World War II	11, 12, 14	12
		1.3.3 describe some of the contributions Canada and Canadians made to the war effort at home during World War I and World War II, as well as some of the effects the wars had on the home from	13	13
		1.3.4 describe the events leading up to the Holocaust and assess Canada's response to those events		
		1.3.5 summarize Canada's role in some key Cold war activities from 1945 to 1989	16	16, 24
		1.3.6 assess some examples of the roles and functions of the Canadian armed forces since 1945, such as peacekeeping and peace making and maintaining security	17, 24	4, 20
2 Change and Continuity	2.1 explain some major ways in which Canada's population has changed since 1914	2.1.1 identify some major groups of immigrants that have come to Canada since 1914 and describe the circumstances that led to their immigration	2, 15	15, 19
		2.1.3 explain some of the ways in which the lives of adolescents, women, and seniors have changed since World War I as a result of major demographic shifts and social changes		
		2.1.4 describe the changing impact of the baby boom generation on Canadian society from the 1950's to the present	19	22

	2.2 evaluate the impact of some technological developments on Canadians in different periods	2.2.1 explain how some key technological developments have changed the everyday lives of Canadians since World War I	18, 20, 21	
		2.2.2 explain how some key technological innovations in military and other fields have changed the way war has been planned and fought, and describe their impact on combatants and civilians		
		2.2.3 describe the effects of selected scientific and technological innovations developed by Canadians	22	26
	2.3 describe changes in Canada's international status and its role in the world since 1914	2.3.1 identify changes in Canada's international status since World War I	26	27
		2.3.2 describe Canada's responses to some of the major human tragedies that have occurred since World War I	1	28
		2.3.3 describe the development of Canada's role as a world leader in defending human rights since World War II	4, 25	29
		2.3.4 summarize Canada's changing relationship with the United States	3, 26	30
3 Citizenship and Heritage	3.1 describe the impact of significant social and political movements on Canadian society	3.1.1 summarize the key contribution of women's movements in Canada since 1914	28	31, 33
		3.1.2 identify key struggles and contribution of the labour movement in Canada as well as key contributions of selected labour leaders	27	23, 32
		3.1.3 describe some of the factors shaping the experience of Aboriginal peoples in Canada since 1914 and ways in which Aboriginal people have worked to achieve recognition of Aboriginal and treaty rights	30	21
		3.1.4 compare the different beliefs and values of selected political parties that emerged out of political movements	32, 44	

	3.2 describe how individual Canadians have contributed to the development of Canada and its emerging sense of identity	3.2.1 describe how selected significant individuals have contributed to the growing sense of Canadian identity since 1914	33, 34	35
		3.2.2 describe how the work of selected artists has reflected Canadian identity	35	36
4 Social, Economic, and Political Structures	4.1 explain changing economic conditions and patterns and how they have affected Canadians	4.1.1 compare economic conditions at selected times in Canada's history and describe their impact on the daily lives of Canadians	29, 37, 38, 40	25, 38, 39
		4.1.2 assess the advantages and disadvantages of American participation in the Canadian economy	3, 39	
		4.1.3 identify some of the major effects of, and concerns arising with, free trade and globalization focusing on at least two groups	6	2, 6
		4.1.4 identify the contributions of selected Canadian entrepreneurs and Canadian owned firms to the development of the Canadian economy	41	40
	4.2 assess the changing role and power of the federal and provincial governments in Canada since 1914	4.2.1 explain why selected social welfare programs were established in Canada	42	
		4.2.2 assess key instances in which the Canadian government chose to restrict citizens' rights and freedoms, in wartime and peacetime	31, 43	
		4.2.3 identify how the federal government has used the media		1, 3

PRACTICE TEST 1

1. According to reports, more than 25 000 000 Sub-Saharan Africans are living with HIV/AIDS. Which of the following actions has the Canadian government taken to help over the last 10 years?
   A. Left it up to the private sector to help out
   B. Asked drug companies to supply low-cost medicine
   C. Sent medical specialists to the hardest hit countries
   D. Committed over $200 million to help fight the problem

2. Which of the following statements about Canada's immigration policy since the end of the Second World War is **true**?
   A. Visible minorities will soon make up the majority of Canada's population.
   B. Canada still has a long way to go before it can be called a tolerant society.
   C. Canadians have become more tolerant of immigrants from around the world.
   D. Canada has a difficult time with foreign policy due to the variety of immigrants.

3. Write a paragraph entitled "The Impact of the Auto Pact" that highlights the key details and specific impact of the pact on the Canadian economy.

   _____
   _____
   _____
   _____

4. Describe why Canada's military involvement with Bosnia in the late 1990s was controversial.

   _____
   _____
   _____
   _____

5. How did the Canadian government deal with potential Nazi war criminals living in Canada in the 1980s?
   A. Had private groups investigate and prepare reports
   B. Identified and extradited them to West Germany for trial
   C. Established a Royal Commission to see if there was a problem
   D. Announced that too much time had passed and no action would be taken

6. List three economic examples of globalization.

_____

_____

_____

_____

Use the following information to answer the next question.

7. Which event is referred to by the newspaper headlines?

   A. Quebec Referendum

   B. Conscription during World War I

   C. Conscription during World War II

   D. The use of the War Measures Act

Use the following information to answer the next question.

A student was preparing a presentation about a political figure in Quebec and came up with the following points:

- early career as a broadcaster
- was a Liberal cabinet minister in the 1960s
- became a leader of the separatist movement
- involved in the introduction of Bill 101

8. The student's presentation is about

   A. Jean Lesage

   B. René Lévesque

   C. Lucien Bouchard

   D. Maurice Duplessis

Use the following information to answer the next question.

One of the most important pieces of legislation passed by the Parti Québécois government was Bill 101, the Charter of the French Language, in 1977. This meant that all signs on all businesses in Quebec had to be in French. Some retailers were not happy with the law. Morton Brownstein, owner of a Montreal shoe store, challenged the law all the way to the Supreme Court of Canada. In 1988, the court decided that English could not be totally prohibited, but that requiring mostly French on commercial signs was a reasonable limit on freedom of expression.

9. Which of the following statements is **true**?

A. Quebec accepts Supreme Court of Canada decisions.

B. Quebec wants English education banned in the province.

C. Quebec's business community unanimously supported Bill 101.

D. Quebec would like to hold a conference on bilingualism in Canada.

Use the following information to answer the next question.

10. To what event do the newspaper headlines refer?

A. World War I

B. World War II

C. The Cold War

D. The Korean War

Use the following information to answer the next question.

A grade 10 Social Studies class was given an assignment for which students could choose one of the following topics:

I   Dieppe

II Hong Kong

III Juno Beach

IV National Resources Mobilization Act

11. All of these topics involve Canada

    A. during World War I

    B. during World War II

    C. following World War I

    D. following World War II

Use the following information to answer the next question.

He was born in 1915 in Manitoba. When World War II broke out, he signed up several times to fight with the Canadian Army, but he was not accepted because he was Aboriginal. Eventually, he was accepted. His unit, an elite squad trained to be paratroopers, had received intense instruction in stealth tactics, hand-to-hand combat, the use of explosives for demolition, amphibious warfare, rock climbing, and mountain fighting. In full view of German soldiers, he pretended to be a farmer weeding his crops in order to repair a communications wire. For this, he was awarded the Military Medal. He spent three days behind enemy lines, and four German units, including their artillery, were knocked out of action.

12. This passage refers to

    A. Elijah Harper

    B. Tommy Prince

    C. Harold Cardinal

    D. Matthew Coon Come

13. The **most controversial** action taken by the Canadian munitions industry during World War II was

    A. spending $10 billion

    B. producing 16 000 aircraft

    C. producing synthetic rubber

    D. providing uranium for the Manhattan Project

14. Which of the following statements regarding the firebombing of Dresden during World War II is **most accurate**?

   A. Canada chose not to be involved.

   B. Canada's pilots flew on many of the missions.

   C. Canada was only involved in maintenance and communication.

   D. Canada was as involved as the other Allies but apologized after the war.

15. Which of the following objectives listed in the 1978 Immigration Act could **best** be used as evidence that Canada accepts refugees regardless of colour, religion, or ethnicity?

   A. Non-discrimination

   B. Reuniting of families

   C. Promotion of Canada's economic and social goals

   D. International obligation to provide a safe haven for refugees

16. In which of the following Cold War conflicts that involved the United States did the Canadian military have an official role?

   A. Korean War

   B. Vietnam War

   C. Central America

   D. Cuban Missile Crisis

17. Describe at least three activities that Canada's Armed Forces are involved with on a regular basis.

   _____

   _____

   _____

   _____

18. Which of the following statements about where Canadians live is **most accurate**?

   A. About 50% of Canadians live in urban areas and 50% live in rural areas.

   B. Close to 80% of Canadians live in rural or suburban areas to be close to work.

   C. It varies from province to province, but the split is about 65% urban, 35% rural.

   D. Close to 80% of Canadians live in urban or suburban areas to be close to work.

Use the following information to answer the next question.

Statistics About Baby Boomers
- Over 50% of baby boomers do not exercise.
- Rates of obesity among baby boomers have soared by nearly 60%.
- Baby boomers between ages 45 and 60 are less fit than seniors over the age of 60.
- Today, 21% of baby boomers are smokers compared to 29% a decade ago.

19. Which of the following sentences **best** summarizes this information about baby boomers?

A. They need more exercise.

B. They smoke less than seniors.

C. Their life expectancy is going down.

D. They are healthier than the previous generation.

20. List three services related to transportation infrastructure that are run by the government.

_____

_____

_____

_____

Use the following information to answer the next question.

In a panel discussion about the effects of technology on working conditions, the following speakers made these points:

Speaker I   We used to work eight hours a day and half a day on Saturdays. Everything was closed on Sundays. Mothers stayed home with the kids, and the kids turned out pretty good. They're the ones in charge of the world today.

Speaker II   It sounded like it was better in the old days, but there were all kinds of problems people don't want to talk about. My dad was always working, and when he wasn't, he was tired. My wife and I each work a 35-hour week, and we're able to spend a lot of time with the kids.

Speaker III   It's great that some people work fewer hours than before, but I don't think they spend their time off with their kids. A lot of people are actually working longer hours than we used to work, and they are just so much busier. With both parents needing to work, kids today are getting into more trouble than ever before.

Speaker IV   One thing is for sure about work today; for the most part, you need an education or training to make decent money. A lot of my dad's friends did not even finish high school but worked long hard hours and created successful businesses. I will do whatever I can to ensure my kids get a post-secondary education.

21. Which speakers believe that new technology has made working conditions worse than they used to be?

   A. Speakers I and II

   B. Speakers I and III

   C. Speakers I, II, and III

   D. Speakers I, II, III, and IV

Use the following information to answer the next question.

A student wrote the following about the Avro Arrow:

In 1953, Canada's Liberal government authorized A.V. Roe of Canada to produce a jet fighter, which was to be called the Avro Arrow. Two prototypes were to be built, and over 14 000 aerospace jobs were created. When the prototypes were completed, tests indicated that this jet could fly at nearly twice the speed of sound; however, the production cost was supposed to be $2 million and the actual costs had skyrocketed to $12.5 million.

22. Which of the following sentences **best** concludes this paragraph?

   A. The company was sold to American-owned Boeing.

   B. The Arrow made A.V. Roe and Company a lot of money.

   C. On its final test, the Arrow crashed, and the project was cancelled.

   D. The new Conservative government of Canada cancelled the project.

23. Which of the following statements about Canadian sovereignty granted by the Statute of Westminster in 1931 is **true**?

   A. The constitution was immediately amended.

   B. Foreign affairs would still be directed by Britain.

   C. The British Privy Council would be the final court of appeal.

   D. The position of governor general was created to represent the monarch.

Use the following information to answer the next question.

Keeping the peace demands courage and sacrifice. Canada knows well that courage and sacrifice. The efforts of over 125 000 Canadian peacekeepers in the past half century have not been without cost: 114 Canadians have died on UN peace operations—more per capita than any other country. In all, 2 355 brave men and women have paid the ultimate price for peace while serving on UN missions. They wore the flags of 114 nations, but they served under one banner, that of the United Nations. Their deaths are a reminder that just as peacekeepers have a responsibility to protect the most vulnerable, so governments have a responsibility to support peacekeepers, to help them do their work and to ensure their safety.

Fifty years ago, Canada's then-Foreign Minister, Lester Pearson, was awarded the 1957 Nobel Peace Prize, in large part for his role in making peacekeeping a reality. When Pearson called for "a truly international peace and police force" to stand between the combatants and defuse the Suez crisis, that was something new.

Peace operations have since come to epitomize the values of the United Nations: coming together, rising above national interests, and working for the common good. Today, the UN has over 100 000 courageous civilians, soldiers, and police officers on peace operations around the world. Regional organizations have a further 75 000 personnel deployed under UN mandates. Such a level of demand and diversity of missions is unprecedented.

In closing, I'd like to pass on a message from that veteran peacekeeper, Colonel Ethell.

"We all have an obligation to the international community," he said. "We can't turn our backs on it. So don't quit."

24. Which of the following statements **best** describes the speaker's view of Canada's role in peacekeeping?

A. Peacekeeping has always been successful.

B. Canadians are obligated to keep up the good work.

C. The demand for peacekeepers is slowly diminishing.

D. Peacekeeping missions have cost too many lives, and it is time to stop.

25. Describe two areas identified by Amnesty International that Canada needs to examine carefully.

_____

_____

_____

_____

Use the following information to answer the next question.

For a law to be enacted, it must first be adopted by the House of Commons and the Senate before being signed by the governor general, which is simply a formality. In 1987, Prime Minister Brian Mulroney passed the Free Trade Agreement (FTA) with the United States in the House of Commons; however, the Liberal-controlled Senate did not pass it.

26. The result of the Senate not passing the FTA was that

A. the governor general signed it anyway

B. Brian Mulroney campaigned on it in 1988 and won a majority government

C. the Liberals campaigned against it in 1988 and won a minority government

D. the Mulroney government asked for a Supreme Court decision, and they accepted the FTA

27. Describe **two** key details about the Canadian Labour Congress.

_____

_____

_____

_____

Use the following information to answer the next question.

A student doing research on the Famous Five came up with the following points:

I   One of the five became the British Empire's first female judge.

II They wanted women to be allowed to be senators.

III They all served in the Alberta legislature.

IV One of the Famous Five became the first woman senator.

28. Which two of the given statements are **incorrect**?

A. I and II

B. II and III

C. II and IV

D. III and IV

Use the following information to answer the next question.

A teacher wrote these points on the board:
- promoted natural resource development
- constructed the St. Lawrence Seaway
- built the Trans-Canada Highway

29. Which Canadian prime minister is associated with these activities?

    A. Lester Pearson

    B. Mackenzie King

    C. Louis St. Laurent

    D. John Diefenbaker

30. List **three** important points about the Assembly of First Nations.

_____

_____

_____

_____

31. Describe **three** interesting points about the Canadian Civil Liberties Association.

_____

_____

_____

_____

32. Which of the following parties are considered right of centre?

    A. Cooperative Commonwealth Federation and Social Credit

    B. Cooperative Commonwealth Federation and Reform

    C. Social Credit and Progressive

    D. Social Credit and Reform

33. Give a brief biography of Arthur Currie.

_____

_____

_____

_____

Use the following information to answer the next question.

This hockey hall of famer was the first to score 50 goals in 50 games in a National Hockey League season and the first to score 500 goals in a career. While he played for his team, they won the Stanley Cup eight times. He also was a winner of the Hart Trophy as the most valuable player in the NHL. In a playoff game against the Toronto Maple Leafs, he scored all five goals for his team in a 5-1 victory and was named all three stars.

34. Which hockey player is referred to in the given passage?

 A. Gordie Howe

 B. Mark Messier

 C. Wayne Gretzky

 D. Maurice Richard

35. Describe **three** important details about Michael Ondaatje.

_____

_____

_____

_____

36. Give a point form biography of Pierre Elliot Trudeau.

_____

_____

_____

_____

Use the following information to answer the next question.

There was no comparison in the way people lived between these two decades. In one of them, people had the ability to enjoy new technology, in the other, people were struggling to feed their families. In one of them, people were enjoying their leisure time, in the other, people spent their time looking for work to pay the bills. In one of them, production went to unprecedented levels, in the other, productivity declined dramatically.

37. Which two decades are referred to in the passage?

 A. 1910s and 1920s

 B. 1920s and 1930s

 C. 1930s and 1940s

 D. 1940s and 1950s

Use the following information to answer the next question.

The Canadian economy enjoyed growth like never before after World War II. While two-thirds of Canadians were in the poor category in 1941, only one-third were considered poor in 1951. One of the reasons for the prosperity was the international demand for raw materials. This in turn led to Canadian demand for housing and other consumer products. Because there were low rates of unemployment, social programs, such as unemployment insurance, were discontinued. However, wages were high, and the dream of owning a home, a car, and sending kids to post-secondary educational institutions became a reality for many by the 1960s.

38. In point form, list **three** important details about the Canadian economy after World War II.

_____

_____

_____

_____

Use the following information to answer the next question.

At a panel discussion on the Canadian economy, the following speakers made these opening statements:

Speaker I   We are going to lose control of the economy; the profits mostly go to the United States.

Speaker II   Our neighbour to the south has sped up the development of our economy; they are risk takers.

Speaker III If we continue to allow foreign investment, Canadians are at risk of losing some of the things that make them unique.

Speaker IV   I would be more worried if the cultural differences were insurmountable; we have a lot in common with them.

39. Which two speakers would **most** favour American involvement in the Canadian economy?

A. Speakers I and II

B. Speakers II and III

C. Speakers II and IV

D. Speakers III and IV

40. Which of the following pairs of provinces have generally enjoyed prosperity since the end of World War II?

A. Alberta and Ontario

B. Quebec and Ontario

C. Newfoundland and Ontario

D. Saskatchewan and Ontario

Use the following information to answer the next question.

A student doing a research project on a particular company came up with the following information:

- formed in 1925 in Quebec
- provides services to homes and industries around the world
- by 1960, oil and gas accounted for over 33% of its value, finance accounted for 11%, and pulp and paper for 10%
- owns many insurance companies, such as London Life and Great West Life
- revenues for 2007 were close to $30 billion
- has many political ties in Canada

41. The company referred to in the passage is

A. Quebecor

B. Ontario Hydro

C. Canadian Pacific Railway

D. Power Corporation of Canada

42. In 1935, during the Depression, Prime Minister Richard B. Bennett introduced his version of the New Deal. Describe this deal and the country's reaction to it.

_____

_____

_____

_____

43. Canada rationed, censored, conscripted, and interned those deemed enemies during World War II. Which of the following points would a member of the Canadian Civil Liberties Association **most likely** agree with?

A. People's rights should never be taken away.

B. As long as people's rights are restored after the war, it is not a big problem.

C. While interning enemy aliens is acceptable, forcing Canadians to go to war is not.

D. Sometimes, it is necessary for governments to assume emergency powers temporarily.

Use the following information to answer the next question.

In the late 1980s and for most of the 1990s, provincial and federal governments embraced the idea that they were spending too much. This overspending created a deficit and compiled into a debt that had to be addressed. The premier of Alberta, Ralph Klein, the premier of Ontario, Mike Harris, and the prime minister of Canada, Brian Mulroney, were leaders in reducing government expenditure in the area of social programs. Hospital emergency room waits became longer, average class sizes became larger, and those who rely on government transfer payments, such as unemployment insurance, disability insurance, or pensions, saw their real income decline.

44. Which of the following political parties would **most** disagree with this policy?

   A. Liberal Party

   B. Bloc Québécois

   C. Conservative Party

   D. New Democratic Party

45. Explain how Canada has a heterogeneous population.

_____

_____

_____

_____

ANSWERS AND SOLUTIONS FOR PRACTICE TEST 1

1. D	13. D	25. OR	37. B
2. C	14. B	26. B	38. OR
3. OR	15. A	27. OR	39. C
4. OR	16. A	28. D	40. A
5. C	17. OR	29. C	41. D
6. OR	18. D	30. OR	42. OR
7. B	19. A	31. OR	43. A
8. B	20. OR	32. D	44. D
9. A	21. B	33. OR	45. OR
10. A	22. D	34. D	
11. B	23. C	35. OR	
12. B	24. B	36. OR	

1. D

The government of Canada has spent over $200 million and continues to spend to help fight the problem. As a result of this help from Canada and other developed nations, progress is being made in reducing the spread of HIV/AIDS.

2. C

Canada's immigration policy has changed greatly since the end of World War II. For a variety of reasons, such as economic need or taking in refugees, Canada has become more multicultural.

3. Open Response

In the 1960s, the Auto Pact was reached between Canada and the United States. In 1964, less than 10% of vehicles made in Canada were sent to the U.S. By 1968, 60% of Canadian vehicles made were shipped to the U.S. In 1970, Canada registered a small auto trade surplus with the U.S. for the first time. Between 1965 and 2002, the number of people employed in this industry rose from 75 000 to 491 000. Vehicles accounted for 12% of Canadian manufacturing GDP in 2002. The agreement was abolished in 2001.

4. Open Response

While NATO had permission from the UN to help implement the peace agreement, there was no UN approval for bombing, only for implementing and stabilizing the Daytona Peace Accord. The bombings in May and June 1999 raised issues regarding the original NATO agreement, which was based on mutual defence, not attack.

5. C

In 1985, Progressive Conservative Prime Minister Brian Mulroney created the Commission of Inquiry on War Criminals in Canada, often referred to as the Deschênes Commission. While the commission identified over 770 potential war criminals, by 1995, none had actually been prosecuted. Since 2001, three Nazi war criminals have been convicted in Canada.

6. Open Response

There are many examples of globalization in today's economy. Three examples are:
1) purchasing fruit grown in other countries,
2) bringing in immigrants to fill jobs, and
3) entering into free trade agreements.

7. B

The newspaper headlines refer to the issue of conscription during World War I.

At this time, the conscription issue was very volatile. Quebecers vehemently opposed it. The Borden Conservative government passed the Military Voters Act in 1917, giving soldiers and military nurses the right to vote. Women at home who had close male relatives serving in the war were also allowed to vote. Votes were taken away from immigrants from enemy nations, and many Conservative supporters suggested that voting for the Laurier Liberals was a vote for Germany (against Canada).

8. B

The presentation is about René Lévesque. Jean Lesage was the Quebec premier during the Quiet Revolution of 1960 to 1966. Lucien Bouchard formed the Bloc Québécois in 1990 following the failed ratification of the Meech Lake Accord. Maurice Duplessis was Quebec's premier for all but five of the years between 1936 and 1959.

9. A

The true statement is that Quebec accepts Supreme Court decisions.

This passage makes no mention of English education, nor does it suggest that Quebec wanted a conference on bilingualism. The article provides an example of a business not supporting Bill 101.

10. A

These headlines refer to World War I.

The assassination of Austrian Archduke Franz Ferdinand and his wife led Austria to issue an ultimatum to Serbia. The French president vowed revenge against Germany for the humiliation. France suffered in the Franco-Prussian War of 1870. European powers were subjugating Africa in the late 19th and early 20th centuries, causing conflicts among Britain, France, and Germany. Finally, the race between the British and the Germans to build stronger navies was another factor.

11. B

All of these topics involve Canada during World War II.

In 1942, Dieppe was a Canadian attempt to open up the western front for the Allies. Canadians were involved in the unsuccessful attempt to defend the British colony of Hong Kong against Japanese attack in 1941. Canada played a role in the D-Day Invasions on June 6, 1944, which involved 15 000 Canadians at Juno Beach. The National Resources Mobilization Act was introduced by the King government in 1940 to conscript Canadians for home defence only.

12. B

The passage refers to war hero Tommy Prince.

13. D

The most controversial action taken by the Canadian munitions industry was providing uranium for the Manhattan Project. This project's aim was to create the first atomic bombs. The bombs were then used against Japan in August 1945.

14. B

Canada participated in the bombings of Dresden as part of the overall Allied strategy of forcing Germany to surrender without preconditions.

15. A

The point regarding non-discrimination best exemplifies Canada's commitment to accept immigrants regardless of race, colour, or ethnicity.

16. A

Canada's military was involved in the Korean War from 1950 to 1953.

Canada's military did not have an official role in the Vietnam War (1950s to 1970s), or in the Cuban Missile Crisis (1962). During the 1980s, despite his close relationship with U.S. President Ronald Reagan, Prime Minister Brian Mulroney did not support his policies in Central America.

17. Open Response

Canada's Armed Forces are involved in many activities on a regular basis. Some of those are:
1) providing vital survival services such as search and rescue, 2) helping Canadians during a domestic or environmental crisis, 3) assisting other government departments in the fight against illegal drugs, and 4) serving in NATO and UN missions.

18. D

Like the citizens of most industrialized countries, almost 80% of Canadians live in urban or suburban areas.

19. A

The best sentence is that baby boomers need more exercise. Exercise is a control for obesity and promotes better fitness and life expectancy.

While the life expectancy of baby boomers may be going down, the information provided does not state this explicitly.

20. Open Response

There are several services related to transportation infrastructure that are run by the government. Three of those are:

1. Maintaining roads, highways, and bridges
2. Ensuring that ports and harbours are maintained
3. Building roads and sewers for new communities

21. B

Speakers I and III like the idea that in the past there was a parent who stayed at home and the kids got into less trouble. They believe that people are busier today than they were in the past.

Speakers II and IV tend to be positive about the changes.

22. D

The Avro Arrow project was cancelled in 1959 by Prime Minister John Diefenbaker's Conservative government because of costs. This was a controversial decision because the monetary penalty for cancelling was about the same as it would have been to complete the project entirely.

23. C

Canada was not given the authority to have its Supreme Court as the final court of appeal until 1949; until then, this was the job of the British Privy Council. Canada did, however, assume full control over foreign affairs and has had a governor general since 1867. The constitution was not amended and ratified until 1982.

24. B

The speaker believes Canadians cannot turn their backs on the international community. He or she also states that the number of people involved in peacekeeping is 175 000 and the demand for peacekeepers continues to grow.

25. Open Response

Amnesty International has identified several issues related to women in federal prisons in Canada. They would also like to see the land claim disputes with Aboriginals resolved. They also believe that any democratic nation that conducts foreign trade with a non-democratic nation, such as China, is endorsing the human rights policies of that nation.

26. B

The Free Trade Agreement issue was about closer ties to the United States. The 1988 election was about the FTA, and Mulroney won a majority government.

The governor general does not have the option to sign a bill that is not passed by both houses of Parliament.

27. Open Response

The Canadian Labour Congress was founded in the 1950s. It has approximately 3 000 000 members. Most Canadian unions are affiliated with it.

28. D

Statements III and IV are incorrect. Three of the Famous Five served in the Alberta legislature, but the first woman senator was not among them.

Emily Murphy was the British Empire's first female judge. The Famous Five's fight was for women to be declared "persons" and become eligible for Senate appointments.

29. C

During the St. Laurent era (1948–1957), Canada's economy enjoyed prosperity. The government promoted economic growth and opportunity by building the St. Lawrence Seaway and the Trans-Canada Highway.

30. Open Response

The National Indian Brotherhood became the Assembly of First Nations in 1982. It represents Status Indians and First Nations people in Canada. It opposed the Meech Lake Accord because the needs of Aboriginal people were neglected, but it supported the Charlottetown Accord because it would have given Aboriginals self-government.

31. Open Response

The Canadian Civil Liberties Association is completely funded by private individuals; they do not want government money because they frequently find themselves in disputes with the government when they feel Canadians' fundamental freedoms are being compromised.

The Canadian Civil Liberties Association favours the right to public demonstrations. They opposed the use of the War Measures Act in 1970. They favour freedom of speech even when some consider it offensive.

32. D

The Social Credit and the Reform Party are to the right of centre.

The Progressive Party, born after World War I, was created due to farmer discontent and also had a base in Ontario. The Cooperative Commonwealth Federation is to the left of centre.

33. Open Response

Arthur Currie did not serve in government; he did, however, establish a reputation as a "brilliant military commander," according to British Prime Minister Lloyd George, despite starting off without any military experience. He led the Canadian Corps at the Battle of Passchendaele.

34. D

Maurice Richard was the first NHL player to score 50 goals in 50 games and the first to score 500 goals in a career.

35. Open Response

Michael Ondaatje was born in Sri Lanka and came to Canada in 1962. He received the Governor General's Award for poetry in 1970. The movie *The English Patient* was based on his work and won nine Academy Awards. In 2007, he received his fifth Governor General's Literary Award.

36. Open Response

Pierre Elliot Trudeau:

 – led his party in five elections

 – introduced the National Energy Program that angered the West, especially Alberta

 – repatriated the constitution

 – was an MP in Quebec during one of the Quebec referenda

37. B

The passage refers to the 1920s and the 1930s. In general terms, the 1920s were a time of prosperity for many, while the 1930s, the decade during which the Great Depression occurred, are referred to as the Dirty Thirties, as many people were unemployed and unable to support themselves and their families during this time.

38. Open Response

After World War II, the economic lives of Canadians greatly improved.

 – The demand for consumer products was high.

 – Following World War II, Canadians enjoyed prosperity.

 – Attending university was now possible for more people.

 – Unemployment was low.

 – People were more easily able to own a home and a car.

39. C

Speakers II and IV emphasize the positive aspects of American involvement in the economy. Speaker II states that American investors have taken some economic risks that Canadian investors were not willing to take. Speaker IV seems to believe that Canadians have so much in common with the U.S. that there is nothing to lose.

40. A

Alberta has been prosperous because of the presence of oil and gas. Ontario has many natural resources, and Southern Ontario has been at the centre of Canadian manufacturing.

One of the reasons that Quebec has not had even growth is the fear investors had regarding possible separation. Newfoundland and Saskatchewan have also had economic ups and downs, as their economies were based on the primary industries of fishing and agriculture, respectively. Recently, both of these provinces have seen improvements due to the presence of natural resources such as oil and gas, which are in demand.

41. D

The information refers to the Power Corporation of Canada. It is among the top 25 companies in Canada in terms of profits in 2006.

42. Open Response

The new Liberal government led by Prime Minister Mackenzie King created a Royal Commission (Rowell-Sirois), which recommended that the federal government be given control over pensions and unemployment insurance. The provinces, especially Ontario and Quebec, were not pleased with their loss of power.

Bennett's New Deal was an effort to spend money on programs that the Court felt were provincial responsibilities. Bennett lost the 1935 election largely because of the economic problems Canadians faced.

43. A

The Canadian Civil Liberties Association (CCLA) would most likely agree with the position that people's rights should never be taken away.

It would not support interning "enemy aliens" such as the Japanese. The CCLA worked very hard to have the Canadian government apologize to the people who were interned and compensate them.

44. D

The New Democratic Party would most disagree with this policy because they have always supported social programs and higher taxes, especially for upper income earners and big businesses.

45. Open Response

A heterogeneous population is a population consisting of many different cultural, ethnic, and religious groups.

There are numerous ethnocultural, religious, and linguistic groups that make up the multicultural society and heterogeneous population of Canada. All Canadians, except for Aboriginal peoples, originally came from other parts of the world. These groups have all made important contributions to the development and growth of Canada as a sovereign nation.

PRACTICE TEST 2

Use the following information to answer the next question.

1. Give a point form summary of facts about the Canadian Broadcasting Corporation (min. 3).

   _____

   _____

   _____

   _____

2. Explain how **two** of the following three examples show the Canadian government promoting economic opportunity since World War II.

   A. Trans-Canada Highway

   B. North American Free Trade Agreement

   C. Funding for venues to host international events

   _____

   _____

   _____

   _____

Use the following information to answer the next question.

A student doing a summary of a Canadian institution wrote the following passage:

This Crown corporation was formed in 1936 because the 1929 Aird Commission had concerns regarding American influence on Canadian culture. Some of its funding is through the government; however, it does generate income on its own. Its cultural influence began to decline in the 1980s because of federal budget cuts and competition, which is less regulated.

3. Which institution is described in this passage?

   A. Canadian Radio-television and Telecommunications Commission

   B. Canadian Broadcasting Corporation

   C. Canadian Council for the Arts

   D. National Film Board

Use the following information to answer the next question.

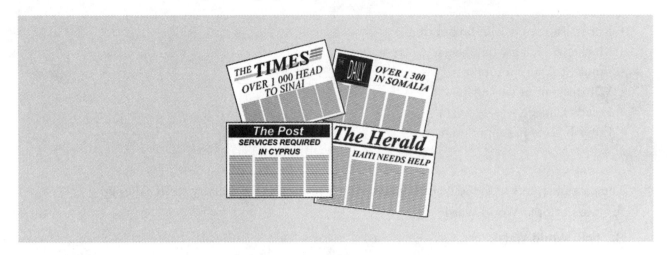

4. Which of the following sentences explains what the newspaper headlines have in common?
    A. Canada has sent foreign aid to each of the places
    B. The Canadian military fought wars in these places
    C. Canada sent United Nations peacekeepers to these places
    D. Canadian volunteers went to these places for humanitarian missions

5. Which of the following statements **best** describes Canada's involvement in war and peacekeeping?
    A. The United States has always acted before Canada
    B. As a rule, Canada has acted with Britain and Western Europe
    C. Canada only acts if both the U.S. and Western Europe take action
    D. Canadian involvement is independent of the U.S. and Western Europe

6. Describe three roles of the World Trade Organization.

    _____

    _____

    _____

    _____

7. Describe the foreign policies of Canada and the United States toward Europe between the two World Wars.

    _____

    _____

    _____

    _____

- Robert Borden was in favour of it
- Mackenzie King would use it if necessary
- Louis St. Laurent supported his leader
- Wilfrid Laurier was against it
- French Canada was against it
- English Canada supported it

8. The passage refers to the issue of Canada using conscription for military service during

   A. wars prior to World War I

   B. both World Wars

   C. World War II

   D. World War I

9. Describe the Quiet Revolution.

   _____

   _____

   _____

   _____

10. Contrast the Meech Lake Accord with the Charlottetown Accord.

    _____

    _____

    _____

    _____

11. List any **two** events that were partial causes for the beginning of World War II.

    _____

    _____

    _____

    _____

Use the following information to answer the next question.

The task was given to the Canadian Corps under the command of Sir Arthur William Currie. On April 9, 1917, 20 000 soldiers attacked; by April 12, the Allies were successful in gaining control of the hill. There were 10 602 Canadian casualties, including 3 598 deaths. Four Canadians received the Victoria Cross—the highest military honour awarded for courage and bravery in the face of enemy danger to members of the military from any British Commonwealth country.

12. To which famous war battle does this passage refer?

    A. Ypres

    B. Dieppe

    C. Hong Kong

    D. Vimy Ridge

13. Which of the following activities was **not** directly associated with Canadian involvement in World War II?

    A. Camp X

    B. Halifax Explosion

    C. British Commonwealth Air Training

    D. Over a quarter of a million women working in the munitions industry

14. Describe the events in Nanking in 1937.

    _____

    _____

    _____

    _____

15. Describe the three goals of the 1978 Immigration Act and how each of these goals was important for Canada as a nation.

    _____

    _____

    _____

    _____

16. The North American Air Defence Command is **best** defined as an agreement involving

    A. Canada and the United States

    B. The NATO countries in air defence

    C. Canada, Britain, and the United States

    D. Canada, the United States, and Mexico

Use the following information to answer the next question.

The launch of Canada's RADARSAT-2 on December 14, 2007, was so successful that the Department of National Defence's Polar Epsilon project will be taking on another project to strengthen Canada's sovereignty in the Arctic. This new space-based initiative will cost $60 million, and it will provide enhanced land and sea surveillance capabilities for the Canadian Forces at home and abroad. The initiative will also support Canadian Forces sovereignty patrols and operations and strengthen Canada's presence in the North. Improved surveillance capabilities will allow a more efficient and timely Canadian Forces' response to domestic and foreign affairs and search and rescue operations. Currently, Polar Epsilon augments the Canadian military presence in the Arctic. This presence underscores the government's objective of fostering a healthy and prosperous northern region within a strong and sovereign Canada.

17. After reading the above paragraph, list **three** of Canada's goals.

_____

_____

_____

_____

18. State at least **two** different groups that immigrated to Canada in large numbers in the 20th century and give approximate timeframes for that immigration.

_____

_____

_____

_____

Use the following information to answer the next question.

Speaker I   Our economy cannot create jobs fast enough to accommodate everybody.

Speaker II   Too many immigrants end up relying on welfare programs.

Speaker III New immigrants take jobs away from Canadians who already live here.

Speaker IV   It's all right as long as they speak English or French; teaching a new language is expensive.

19. Which speakers promote the traditional, early 20th-century beliefs that reflected Canada's policies toward immigration?

A. Speakers I and II

B. Speakers III and IV

C. Speakers I, II, and III

D. Speakers I, II, III, and IV

20. The primary role of the United Nations Security Council is to

   A. decide questions involving international law

   B. coordinate the daily work of United Nations' agency staff

   C. provide a public forum for debate among all member nations

   D. create and oversee United Nations' peacekeeping operations

21. Describe three major issues facing Canada's Aboriginals today.

_____

_____

_____

_____

Use the following information to answer the next question.

A student came up with some interesting comparisons between 1950 and 1960. This is what she found had occurred in Canada during that period:

- hot dog production rose from 750 million pounds to 1 050 million pounds
- registration in Little League Baseball rose from 776 to 5 700
- potato chip production rose from 320 million pounds to 532 million pounds
- encyclopedia sales rose from $72 million to $300 million
- the percentage of the population between 5 and 14 years old rose from 24.3% to 35.5%

22. Which of the following factors **best** accounts for these changes?

   A. Louis St. Laurent was pressuring corporations to produce more

   B. Changes to Canadian culture were focused on secularization

   C. More immigrants were allowed into the country

   D. The birth rate was skyrocketing

Use the following information to answer the next question.

A student doing a report came up with the following points:

- Over 155 000 manufacturing jobs are in the auto industry
- Economists estimate that for each of these jobs, 7.5 "spinoff" jobs are created
- Canada has the ability to produce 3.5 million vehicles a year
- Between 2000 and 2002, 7 000 autoworker were lost
- The average autoworker earns $27 per hour; spinoff workers earn an average of $22 per hour

23. Which of the following statements is **true**?

   A. Canada sells 3.5 million Canadian-made cars each year.

   B. The loss of 7 000 auto manufacturing jobs would likely mean the loss of over 50 000 other jobs.

   C. Canada's auto industry faces fierce competition from Asian and European carmakers.

   D. Including the "spinoff" jobs, a quarter of a million Canadians owe their livelihood to the auto industry.

24. During the Cold War, many nations achieved independence as a result of

   A. decolonization in Africa and Asia

   B. liberation movements in Latin America

   C. struggles for power among ethnic groups in the Balkans

   D. spheres of influence being established in the Middle East

25. Explain some of the factors that caused the recession that occurred in the 1970s.

   _____

   _____

   _____

   _____

26. Choose **two** of the following famous Canadians and explain what they did to distinguish themselves in the fields of science and technology.

   1. Maude Abbott—medicine

   2. Ursula Franklin—physics

   3. Sir Frederick Banting—medicine

   4. Joseph-Armand Bombardier—technology

Use the following information to answer the next question.

The Balfour Report of 1926 on relations between the self-governing parts of the British Empire was an important document in Canada's evolution to fully self-governing nationhood. The report declared that Britain and the Dominions of Canada, South Africa, Australia, New Zealand and the Irish Free State were to be independent within the British Empire, equal in status in all aspects of their domestic or external affairs.

27. Which of the following statements is **true**?

    A. Canada still does not have total sovereignty

    B. Canada received total sovereignty when the constitution was patriated in 1982

    C. Canada received total sovereignty when the Statute of Westminster was passed in 1931

    D. Canada received total sovereignty when the British Pricy Council ceased to be Canada's final court of appeal in 1949

28. Describe the mission in Somalia that Canada was involved in during the 1990s.

    _____

    _____

    _____

    _____

Use the following information to answer the next question.

A student doing research on a certain document came up with the following information for his report:

- passed by the Canadian parliament while Trudeau was prime minister
- it created the Canadian Human Rights Commission
- passed to ensure that all Canadians enjoy equal opportunities without being hindered by discrimination

29. Which document was the student researching?

    A. Citizenship Act (1977)

    B. Canadian Bill of Rights (1961)

    C. Canadian Human Rights Act (1977)

    D. The Charter of Rights and Freedoms (1982)

30. Choose **one** of the following incidents and describe how it strained relations between Canada and the United States.

    A. 2003 Invasion of Iraq

    B. Voyage of the Manhattan

    C. Creation of the Foreign Investment Review Agency

_____

_____

_____

_____

Use the following information to answer the next question.

It began in 1967, when Liberal Prime Minister Lester Pearson responded to a campaign by a coalition of 32 volunteer groups. The chairperson of the committee was Florence Bird, and some of the members included Jacques Henripin, a professor of demography, John Humphrey, a professor of law, Elsie Gregory MacGill, an aeronautical engineer, and Judge Doris Ogilvie. They produced a 488-page report making 167 recommendations on things such as the Indian Act, family law, daycare, and birth control, to name a few.

31. The given passage is referring to the Royal Commission on

    A. Indian Rights

    B. Human Rights

    C. Aboriginal Peoples

    D. the Status of Women

Use the following information to answer the next question.

I   creation of the Cooperative Commonwealth Federation

II   organizational meeting of the Reform Party

III   organizational meeting of the Progressive Party

IV   riots involving the "On-to-Ottawa Trek" strike leaders

32. Which of the following events occurred in Regina during the Great Depression?

    A. I and II

    B. I and IV

    C. II and IV

    D. II and III

33. Describe the Elizabeth Fry Society of Canada.

_____

_____

_____

_____

34. Which Canadian political party **most** owes its existence to the failure of the Meech Lake Accord?

A. Bloc Québécois

B. Union Nationale

C. Parti Québécois

D. Reform Party of Canada

35. Give a point form biography of Matthew Coon Come.

_____

_____

_____

_____

36. Many Canadian artists have achieved international recognition in different areas. Which of the following Canadians is **not** involved in the performing arts?

A. Karen Kain

B. Dan Aykroyd

C. Oscar Peterson

D. Roberta Bondar

37. Choose **two** of the following political leaders and describe the accomplishments and importance of each.

A. Elijah Harper

B. Tommy Douglas

C. Preston Manning

D. Jacques Parizeau

_____

_____

_____

_____

38. Describe economic life in Canada during the 1920s and 1930s.

_____

_____

_____

_____

Use the following information to answer the next question.

39. The given headlines describe

   A. the development of Canada's economy after World War I

   B. the impact of the baby boom on the Canadian economy

   C. Canada's economy in the 1950s and 1960s

   D. Canada's economy after World War II

Use the following information to answer the next question.

Students were assigned the task of writing an obituary for any person who has made a major contribution to the development of Canada's economy.

Born in Czarist Russia in the 19th century, this man first immigrated to Saskatchewan and later moved to Manitoba, where he was successful in the hotel business. He made vast amounts of money in the liquor business, and by 1965, his product was available in 119 different countries and sales were over $1 billion. For a period of time, one of his sons owned the Montreal Expos baseball team, and his daughter founded the Canadian Centre for Architecture in 1989.

40. Who is being eulogized?

   A. K. C. Irving

   B. Heather Reisman

   C. Samuel Bronfman

   D. Edward Rogers Sr.

ANSWERS AND SOLUTIONS FOR PRACTICE TEST 2

1. OR	11. OR	21. OR	31. D
2. OR	12. D	22. D	32. B
3. B	13. C	23. B	33. OR
4. C	14. OR	24. A	34. A
5. B	15. OR	25. OR	35. OR
6. OR	16. A	26. OR	36. D
7. OR	17. OR	27. C	37. OR
8. D	18. OR	28. OR	38. OR
9. OR	19. D	29. C	39. D
10. OR	20. D	30. OR	40. C

1. **Open Response**

   – The Canadian Broadcasting Corporation (CBC) does broadcast programs that are not made in Canada.

   – It does have a mandate to broadcast mostly Canadian content.

   – Until recently, the CBC has broadcast the Olympics; however, that will change with the 2010 Winter Olympic Games being broadcast by CTV.

   – It is a Crown corporation.

2. **Open Response**

   The government builds and maintains infrastructure, such as the Trans-Canada Highway, so that industries can get their products in and out efficiently.

   International free trade agreements expand the number of potential consumers for industries.

   Government subsidizing of part of the cost for sports venues assisted Montreal in getting the 1976 Summer Olympic Games, Calgary the 1988 Winter Olympic Games, and Vancouver the 2010 Winter Olympic Games. These events bring in tourists from around the world.

3. **B**

   The government makes efforts to promote the Canadian identity as both unique and distinct from the United States. The Canadian Broadcasting Corporation was created in 1936 to present news in both English and French and to provide more Canadian content than was being received from American outlets.

   In 1939, the National Film Board, which produces films that are mostly of a documentary nature about different aspects of Canadian life, was created. The Canada Council for the Arts, established in 1957, gave government grants to artists and scientists, and the Canadian Radio-television and Telecommunications Commission, established in 1968, initially placed controls related to Canadian content on radio and television.

4. **C**

   While it is likely that Canadian foreign aid dollars have been sent to these places and Canadian volunteers have gone in to assist with humanitarian issues, the headlines are all about UN peacekeeping missions. These are only four of over 40 such missions.

5. B

As a rule, Canada has acted with Britain and Western Europe in war and peacekeeping missions. In both WWI and WWII, Canada entered the war before the United States.

6. Open Response

The World Trade Organization tries to ensure that there are rules of trade between different countries, that those rules are followed among member nations, and that developing countries have an opportunity to share in the global prosperity.

7. Open Response

In the interwar period, Canada's foreign policy moved closer to U.S. foreign policy than to British and European foreign policy. Both Canada and the U.S. were isolationist regarding European affairs.

8. D

The issue of compulsory military service (conscription) arose during *both* World War I and World War II. During both wars, French Canadians tended not to support conscription, whereas English Canadians tended to support it.

During World War I, Conservative Prime Minister Robert Borden favoured conscription, but Liberal Opposition Leader Wilfrid Laurier opposed it.

During World War II, Liberal Prime Minister Mackenzie King stated, "Not necessarily conscription, but conscription if necessary." His chief minister from Quebec, Louis St. Laurent, supported King's decision when "limited conscription" was introduced in 1944.

9. Open Response

The Quiet Revolution began after the death of Premier Maurice Duplessis. René Lévesque played an important role as minister of natural resources under Premier Jean Lesage, and hydroelectric facilities were nationalized. The FLQ was created during the Quiet Revolution; however, it was created by individuals who wanted to establish a sovereign Quebec using violence.

10. Open Response

The Meech Lake Accord involved the first ministers of the provinces, while the Charlottetown Accord also included Aboriginal leaders. The Meech Lake Accord was to be ratified by the provinces, while the Charlottetown Accord was to be ratified by referendum. Neither accord was ratified.

11. Open Response

- The rise of Adolf Hitler and his Nazi policies of nationalism and imperialism

- France and Britain's agreement to go to war with Germany if Poland were invaded

- The League of Nations' inability to stop Japanese and Italian aggression in 1931 and 1935, respectively

12. D

The passage is about the Battle of Vimy Ridge during World War I.

Ypres was in 1915 and was the first major battle of World War I involving Canada. Dieppe was an unsuccessful World War II battle in which 5 000 Canadian troops tried to attack Western Europe, and the Battle of Hong Kong in December 1941 involved nearly 2 000 Canadian troops in an unsuccessful attempt to prevent Japan from taking over the British Colony.

13. C

The Halifax Explosion of 1917 killed over 1 600 people and injured nearly 9 000 when a French munitions ship and a Belgian relief vessel collided.

Camp X was a British-run spy school near Whitby, Ontario, that trained spies during World War II.

The British Commonwealth Air Training Program was under the control of the Royal Canadian Air Force. By the end of World War II, 50 000 pilots, 25 000 navigators, and 57 000 other crew members had been trained under this program.

As well, over 250 000 women worked in Canada's arms manufacturing industry.

14. Open Response

The Japanese military invaded Nanking in 1937. An estimated 80 000 women were assaulted. An official military tribunal estimated that over 200 000 civilians and prisoners of war were killed. On several occasions since the 1970s, apologies have been issued to China.

15. Open Response

In 1978, a new Immigration Act had three goals, which were: 1) promoting family reunion, 2) upholding humanitarian values, and 3) encouraging economic growth in Canada. Families were able to immigrate together, creating family ties to Canada. People seeking refuge in Canada were more easily accepted. Immigrants boost the economy by filling jobs and by purchasing in our economy. Because of this new policy, Canada accepted more refugees from all parts of the world and maintained a "zero tolerance" policy for racism.

16. A

The North American Air Defence Command (NORAD) is an agreement between Canada and the United States made in the late 1950s.

17. Open Response

- to ensure that the Canadian Forces have the ability to respond to crises in the Arctic

- to allow a more timely response to search and rescue operations in the Arctic

- to foster a healthy and prosperous northern region within a strong Canada

- to enhance land and sea surveillance

- to strengthen Canada's presence in the North

18. Open Response

- In the early 1920s, Jewish people immigrated because of programs in Russia.

- Close to 200 000 displaced Europeans arrived after World War II (between 1947 and 1952).

- Over 60 000 refugees from Vietnam, Laos, and Cambodia came from 1979 to 1980.

- In 1957, over 35 000 refugees were accepted from Hungary.

19. D

All of the speakers oppose immigration, or, at the very least, they oppose immigrants of different cultures and religions. These ideas tended to be popular opinions until at least after World War II.

20. D

The primary role of the UN Security Council is to initiate and supervise United Nations' peacekeeping operations. It is the role of the International Court of Justice, not the Security Council, to decide questions of international law. The UN Secretariat coordinates the daily work of UN staff. The UN General Assembly provides a forum for debate among all UN member states.

21. Open Response

The suicide rate among Aboriginals tends to be higher than it is in the non-Aboriginal population.

Canada's Aboriginals also have higher rates of drug and alcohol abuse and incarceration. The standard of living among Aboriginals also tends to be lower than it is for non-Aboriginal populations.

22. D

Taken together, this information relates to the short-term impact of the baby boom. Arguably, immigration increased during this period; however, many immigrants were brought in because of the need for workers to service the growing population created by the baby boom.

23. B

Based on the information, if there is one job lost in auto manufacturing, 7.5 would be lost in spinoff jobs. Therefore, when 7 000 jobs were lost (7 000 * 7.5), 52 500 other jobs were lost.

Canada has the ability to *produce* 3.5 million cars a year; it does not say how many are sold. The information provided does not indicate that there is fierce competition from Asian and European car companies.

24. A

From 1945 to 1991, many European colonies in Africa and Asia gained political independence.

Latin America underwent decolonization in the 19th century. Nations in the Balkans (Southeast Europe) gained national sovereignty either prior to World War I or during the 1990s. The establishment of a sphere of influence is a form of imperialism that erodes national sovereignty.

25. Open Response

The 1970s saw a decline in the value of the Canadian dollar, high inflation, and high unemployment. The price of oil increased, meaning increased prices for heating oil, gas, and most products (due to increased production costs). By the end of the decade, the interest rate was almost 20%.

26. Open Response

1) Maude Abbott, one of Canada's earliest female doctors, became an expert in congenital heart disease. 2) Ursula Franklin has a PhD in experimental physics, and her work has helped stop the testing of nuclear weapons in the atmosphere. 3) Sir Frederick Banting discovered insulin to help control diabetes. 4) Joseph-Armand Bombardier is credited with inventing the snowmobile.

27. C

The Balfour Report was used as the basis for the Statute of Westminster, which formally gave the countries mentioned in the passage sovereignty. Canada chose to use the British Privy Council as a final court of appeal until 1949, and patriation of the constitution was not an easy process.

The Liberal government of Prime Minister Pierre Trudeau patriated the constitution in 1982; however, Quebec still has not signed it, despite two attempts by the Progressive Conservative government of Prime Minister Brian Mulroney.

28. Open Response

When Canadians arrived in Somalia to help in 1992, civil war and famine were occurring. Canada sent 845 troops to help disarm the warring population that had already killed 30 000 people. Many people were saved from starvation; however, a 16-year-old boy was tortured to death.

29. C

The Canadian Human Rights Act created the Canadian Human Rights Commission. Its mandate is to investigate claims of discrimination.

30. Open Response

In 2003, when the U.S. invaded Iraq, Canada chose not to become involved, causing tensions between Canada and the United States.

The voyage of the Manhattan, an oil tanker, challenged Canada's sovereignty in the Canadian Arctic.

The Foreign Investment Review Agency made it more difficult for American investors to invest in Canadian industry.

31. D

The Royal Commission on the Status of Women was created in 1967 to recommend steps the government could take to ensure equality for women in the workplace and society in general.

The Royal Commission on Aboriginal Peoples (1996) made some recommendations regarding Aboriginal self-government that have yet to be enacted.

32. B

In 1933, the Regina Manifesto created the Cooperative Commonwealth Federation. In 1935, the On-to-Ottawa Trek leaders held a peaceful demonstration that turned into a violent riot.

The Reform Party emerged in the West in 1987. The Progressive Party formed in 1920 in Ontario and the Prairies and won 64 seats (second behind the Liberals' 117 seats and ahead of the 50 Conservative seats) in the 1921 election.

33. Open Response

The Elizabeth Fry Society was founded in 1939 by Agnes Macphail. Its focus is on helping women in jails and prisons. It is a non-profit organization.

34. A

The Bloc Québécois most owes its existence to the failure of the Meech Lake Accord. It was formed and led by Lucien Bouchard, the minister of the environment in Prime Minister Brian Mulroney's Progressive Conservative government from 1988 to 1990. Bouchard believed that the Meech Lake Accord would satisfy Quebec's needs and, upon its defeat, left the government to form the new party initially made up of members of Parliament from both the Progressive Conservative and Liberal parties.

Both the Parti Québécois and the Union Nationale are involved in Quebec provincial politics.

The Reform Party of Canada, organized and originally led by Preston Manning in the late 1980s, started off as a party based on the notion of Western alienation.

35. Open Response

Matthew Coon Come:

- was born in 1956 and is of Cree descent.
- was the Grand Chief of the AFN from 2000 to 2003
- attended a residential school and later McGill University
- is best known for work opposing the Great Whale Hydroelectric Project at James Bay in Quebec

36. D

Roberta Bondar was the first Canadian woman in space.

Karen Kain is an internationally acclaimed ballerina. Oscar Peterson achieved fame as a jazz pianist. Dan Aykroyd is a comedian.

37. Open Response

Not all of Canada's 20th- and now 21st-century leaders were prime ministers. Some were cabinet ministers, some were provincial premiers, and others were active in the support of specific causes.

Elijah Harper—Manitoba MLA who was not happy with the Meech Lake Accord and prevented the Manitoba legislature from voting on it before the deadline.

Tommy Douglas—CCF premier of Saskatchewan between 1944 and 1961 and an NDP member of Parliament from 1961 to 1971; associated with social programs, especially medicare.

Preston Manning—founder of the Reform Party of Canada in the 1980s due to concerns regarding Western Canada's interests being ignored by the Liberals and Progressive Conservatives.

Jacques Parizeau—the premier of Quebec in 1995. He supported sovereignty and resigned after making inappropriate comments about immigrants following the vote, which the sovereigntists lost.

38. Open Response

As difficult as it was for farmers to make a living in the 1920s, it became almost impossible during the 1930s, especially in the prairies, because of drought. Tariff barriers were also increased all over the world in the 1930s because of the fear that goods from foreign countries would have a negative impact on domestic production and jobs. Unemployment in the late 1920s was relatively low compared to the record levels in the 1930s.

39. D

For a variety of reasons, Canada's economy became prosperous after World War II. New technology in the war led to the production of new consumer goods. People had little to buy during the war, so they had money to spend after the war. As well, the government gave veterans a reduced price for lots on which to buy homes, and because Canada was not attacked during the war, many of the industries and farms operated at peak to produce for both domestic and foreign consumption.

40. C

The obituary applies to Samuel Bronfman. He and his family made a lot of money in hotels and in the liquor business.

Canadian-born Edward Rogers founded a large communications empire. K. C. Irving, also Canadian-born, started in the oil industry before diversifying into other areas. Heather Reisman is president and chief executive officer of Indigo Books, Canada's largest chain.

Appendix

NOTES

GLOSSARY OF TERMS

Aboriginal	First known occupants of a country.
Alliance system	In Europe, alliances between countries were set up to help maintain peace; ironically, these alliances ensured that most of the countries in Europe were drawn into the war.
Amend	To change.
Anglophones	English-speaking people.
Anti-Semitism	Hostility toward or discrimination against Jews as a religious, ethnic, or racial group.
Asylum	A type of protection that is given to refugees by a foreign government.
Autonomy	Total self-government.
Bilingual	Having two languages.
Biotechnology	Using living organisms for new drugs and other things related to medical care.
Boat people	People who seek refugee status by leaving their home country by boat, often in an unsafe vessel; a term that came into use after Vietnamese refugees fled after the Vietnam War.
Canadarm	A device used by space shuttles to manipulate objects in space by remote control.
Capitalism	Private ownership of the means of production.
Closed-door policy	A policy that Canada had of not allowing immigrants from certain countries to settle in Canada.
Cold War	Tensions and hostilities between the former Soviet Union and its allies and the United States and its allies.
Collective security	Keeping international peace.
Concentration camps	A camp where people (as prisoners of war, political prisoners, or refugees) are detained or confined; a place where people who are generally considered undesirable by the state are imprisoned.
Conscription	Forced military service.
Constitution	The basic set of laws in Canada.
Culture	Behaviour and beliefs of a group of people.
D-Day	The successful landing of 130 000 Allied troops in Normandy, France, that opened up the western European theatre of war on June 6, 1944.
Delivery systems	Methods of getting the weapons to the target.
Democratic socialism	Public ownership of the means of production.
Demographers	People who study population trends.
Displaced persons	People forced out of their homeland by war.

Emigrants	People leaving their country.
Espionage	Spying on the enemy.
Ethnic origin	Cultural, racial, and linguistic background of a person.
Ethno-cultural groups	People who share similar national, tribal, or linguistic origins.
Famous Five	A group consisting of Emily Murphy, Henrietta Muir Edwards, Louise McKinney, Irene Parlby, and Nellie McClung. They fought for the recognition of women as persons under the British North America Act. This group of women campaigned in several provinces to help women gain the right to vote.
Fascism	A political philosophy, movement, or regime (as that of the Fascisti) that exalts nation and often race above the individual and stands for a centralized autocratic government headed by a dictatorial leader, severe economic and social regimentation, and forcible suppression of opposition.
Fascist	A government based on dictatorship and strong nationalism.
Federalism	The concept of Quebec remaining part of Canada.
First Nations	All Aboriginals that are not Inuit or Métis.
Foreign Policy	The policy of a sovereign state in its interaction with other sovereign states.
Genocide/Ethnic cleansing	The systematic elimination, usually violently, of a national, racial, or cultural group.
Heterogeneous population	Many different cultural, ethnic, and religious groups in one population.
Holocaust	The genocide of European Jews and others during the Second World War.
Immigrants	People who come to live in another country in which they were not born.
Imperialism	The expansion of one nation's authority over other lands using economic, political, and/or military means.
Industrialized world	The more economically developed countries in the world.
Innovations	New things or methods.
Institutions	Organizations dedicated to a specific purpose.
International War Crimes Tribunals	Courts created to try people charged with war crimes.
Intolerance	A lack of acceptance.
Labour movement	Collective organizations of working people.
Lifestyles	The typical way of life of an individual, group, or culture.
Linguistic groups	Groups speaking different languages as their first language.
Militarism	The build up of military forces for defensive and offensive political desires.

Multicultural society	Many different cultural groups, each making up a significant percentage of the population.
Multiculturalism	A policy of promoting cultural retention rather than assimilation.
Munitions industry	People or companies in the business of making weapons.
National unity	Relieve the tensions between English and French Canada.
Nationalism	A set of principles or a political movement that promotes a nation's political autonomy and national identity based on a shared history or culture, often identified on the grounds of race or ethnicity.
Nationalism	A strong sense of national pride, which often was strengthened by imperialism.
Nationalize	Government takes over ownership.
Nazi	A member of a German fascist party controlling Germany from 1933 to 1945 under Adolf Hitler; a political dictatorship that was nationalistic.
NORAD	North American Aerospace Defense Command; a bi-national United States and Canadian organization charged with the missions of aerospace warning and aerospace control for North America.
North Atlantic Treaty Organization (NATO)	A defence agreement between the United States and its allies; an alliance of 26 countries from North America and Europe committed to fulfilling the goals of the North Atlantic Treaty signed on April 4, 1949.
Nuclear arms race	When two countries compete to build better weapons.
Patriate/ Patriation	Relieve the tensions between English and French Canada.
Pension	A government plan, paid into by the government and working people, that will pay out money for retirement; a private pension plan is paid into by an employee and his/her employer that will pay out money for retirement.
Pogrom	An organized massacre of helpless people, specifically such a massacre of Jews; organized persecution of Jews.
Policies	A high-level overall plan embracing general goals and acceptable procedures, especially of a governmental body.
Quiet Revolution	A time in the 1960s when Quebecers were promoting pride in French-Canadian language and culture.
Racism	Discrimination based on colour, race, religion, or culture.
Referendum	A direct vote by citizens on an issue.
Refugees	People leaving their home country to seek safety in another country.
Religious groups	Groups based on faith.
Repatriate	To restore or return to the country of origin, allegiance, or citizenship. As used in Canadian history, to bring under Canadian rather than British control. To bring the Constitution under Canadian control rather than British control.

Residential schools	Boarding schools for the purpose of trying to assimilate First Nations people.
Rural	People living in the country, usually farmers.
Separatist groups	People who want an independent Quebec.
Social programs	Government programs to assist those in need.
Sovereign nation	An independent country.
Sovereignty	In regards to countries and nations, sovereignty is the ability of a nation to have freedom from external control.
Sovereignty association	Quebec wanted to be an independent country with strong economic ties to the rest of Canada.
Spinster	An unmarried woman (usually past the average age to marry).
Status Indians	First Nations people registered on an official federal list.
Strike	When workers withdraw their services in order to negotiate better working conditions.
Subsidizing	Giving financial assistance.
Suburbs	Outlying areas of cities.
Suffrage/ Franchise	The right to vote.
Traditional political parties	In Canada, the Liberals and the Progressive Conservatives.
Treaty of Versailles	The peace treaty formally ending the First World War.
United Nations	In 1945, representatives of 50 countries met in San Francisco at the United Nations Conference on International Organization to draw up the United Nations Charter. The organization officially came into existence on October 24, 1945, when the Charter had been ratified by China, France, the Soviet Union, the United Kingdom, the United States, and a majority of other signatories. United Nations Day is celebrated on October 24.
Universal Declaration of Human Rights	The basic international pronouncement of the inalienable and inviolable rights of all members of the human family. The declaration was proclaimed in a resolution of the General Assembly on December 10, 1948, as the "common standard of achievement for all peoples and all nations" in respect to human rights. It lists numerous rights—civil, political, economic, social, and cultural—to which people everywhere are entitled.
Urban	People living in cities.
Vimy Ridge	A strategic ridge in northeastern France that gave the Germans a clear view of the battlefield below; April 9–12, 1917.
Widow	A woman whose husband has died.

NOTES

NOTES

NOTES

NOTES

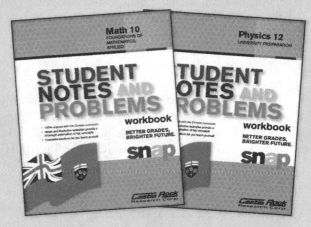

RESOURCE INFORMATION   Order online at www.castlerockresearch.com

THE KEY Study Guides assist in preparing students for course assignments, unit tests, and final or provincial assessments.

KEY Study Guides – $29.95 each plus G.S.T.

SECONDARY	ELEMENTARY
Biology 12, University Prep (SBI4U)	Science 8
Canadian and World Politics 12, University Prep (CPW4U)	Math 7
Chemistry 12, University Prep (SCH4U)	Science 7
English 12, University Prep (ENG4U)	Language 6 Reading & Writing
Math 12 Advanced Functions, University Prep (MHF4U)	Mathematics 6
Math 12 Calculus and Vectors, University Prep (MCV4U)	Science 6
Math 12 Data Management, University Prep (MDM4U)	Math 5
Physics 12, University Prep (SPH4U)	Science 5
World History 12, University Prep (CHY4U)	Mathematics 4
Biology 11, University Prep (SBI3U)	Science 4
Chemistry 11, University Prep (SCH3U)	Language 3 Reading & Writing
English 11, University Prep (ENG3U)	Mathematics 3
Math 11, Foundations for College Mathematics (MBF3C)	Science 3
Math 11, Functions and Applications, U/C Prep (MCF3M)	
Math 11, Functions, University Prep (MCR3U)	
World History 11, University/College Prep (CHW3M)	
Canadian History 10, Academic (CHC2D)	
Canadian History 10, Applied (CHC2P)	
Civics 10, (CHV2O)	
English 10, Academic (ENG2D)	
Math 10, Academic, Principles of Mathematics (MPM2D)	
Math 10, Applied, Foundations of Mathematics (MFM2P)	
OSSLT, Ontario Secondary School Literacy Test	
Science 10, Academic (SNC2D)	
Science 10, Applied (SNC2P)	
English 9, Academic (ENG1D)	
Geography of Canada 9, Academic (CGC1D)	
Math 9, Academic, Principles of Mathematics (MPM1D)	
Math 9, Applied, Foundations of Mathematics (MFM1P)	
Science 9, Academic (SNC1D)	
Science 9, Applied (SNC1P)	

The **Student Notes and Problems (*SNAP*)** workbooks provide complete lessons for course expectations, detailed explanations of concepts, and exercises with complete solutions.

SNAP Workbooks – $29.95 each plus G.S.T.

SECONDARY
Physics 12, University Preparation (SPH4U)
Physics 11, University Preparation (SPH3U)
Math 9, Academic, Principles of Mathematics (MPM1D)
Math 9, Applied, Foundations of Mathematics (MFM1P)

ORDERING OPTIONS
Visit our website at www.castlerockresearch.com

Schools are eligible for an education discount—for more information, contact Castle Rock Research Ontario.

5250 Satellite Drive, Unit 11
Mississauga, ON L4W 5G5
E-mail: Ontario@castlerockresearch.com

Phone: 905.625.3332
Fax: 905.625.3390

Castle Rock
Research Ontario